GCSE
Questions and Answers

BIOLOGY
KEY STAGE 4

Jackie Callaghan & Morton Jenkins

Chief Examiners

SERIES EDITOR: BOB McDUELL

Contents

HOW TO USE THIS BOOK	1
DEVISING A REVISION PLAN	2
DIFFERENT TYPES OF EXAMINATION QUESTION	2
TERMS USED IN QUESTIONS	4
ASSESSMENT OBJECTIVES IN BIOLOGY	5

QUESTIONS AND REVISION SUMMARIES

1	Life processes	7
2	Inheritance and evolution	23
3	Populations and human influences	31
4	Ecosystems	40
5	Human Biology	45
6	Plant Biology	53

ANSWERS	60

Introduction

HOW TO USE THIS BOOK

The aim of the *Questions and Answers* series is to provide students with the help required to attain the highest level of achievement in one of their most important examinations – the General Certificate of Secondary Education (GCSE) or, in Scotland, at General and Credit levels. The books are designed to help all students, up to and including A* grade at GCSE. The series relies on the premise that an experienced Examiner can provide, through examination questions, sample answers and advice, the help students need to secure success. Many revision aids concentrate on providing factual information which might have to be recalled in an examination. This series, while giving factual information in an easy-to-remember form, concentrates on the other skills which need to be developed for new GCSE examinations.

Students often find it useful to plan their revision according to some predetermined pattern, during which weaknesses can be identified and eliminated so that their confidence can grow. Because of this, our primary consideration has been to present the main principles on which study can be based.

The *Questions and Answers* series is designed to provide:

- Easy-to-use **Revision Summaries** which identify important factual information. These are to remind you, in summary form, of the topics you will need to have revised in order to answer exam questions.

- Advice on the different types of question in each subject and how to answer them well to obtain the highest marks.

- Information about other skills, apart from the recall of knowledge, that will be tested on examination papers. These are sometimes called **Assessment Objectives**. Modern GCSE examinations put great emphasis on the testing of objectives other than knowledge and understanding. Typically, questions testing these Assessment Objectives can make up 50% of the mark allocated to the written papers. Assessment Objectives include communication, problem solving, evaluation and interpretation. The *Questions and Answers* series is intended to develop these skills by the use of questions and showing how marks are allocated.

- Many examples of **examination questions**, with spaces for you to fill in your answers, just as on an examination paper. Students can improve by studying a sufficiently wide range of questions, providing they are shown the way to improve their answers to these questions. It is advisable that students try these questions first before going to the answers and the advice which accompanies the answers. Some of the questions come from actual examination papers or specimen materials issued by Examination Boards. Other questions have been written to mirror closely these questions. The writing has been done by Chief Examiners who write questions for Examination Boards. The questions meet the requirements of all British Examination Boards.

- **Sample answers** to all of the questions.

- **Advice from Examiners**. By using the experience of actual Chief Examiners we are able to give advice which can enable students to see how their answers can be improved and success ensured.

Success in GCSE examinations comes from proper preparation and a positive attitude to the examination, developed through a sound knowledge of facts and an understanding of principles. These books are intended to overcome 'examination nerves' which often come from a fear of not being properly prepared.

Introduction

DEVISING A REVISION PLAN

The importance of beginning your revision well in advance of your examination cannot be overemphasized. You will obtain a fair idea of your memory capacity by reading a part of a text which is new to you and, after 40 minutes, writing out how many of the facts you can remember. The average person will recall about 50%, then after an interval of 10 minutes, 25% of the original material will be remembered. After two days you will probably recall no more than 15%. These are average figures, of course, so do not be depressed if your scores are lower, or complacent if they are higher. Your capacity for retention will be influenced by the amount of sleep that you have had, what other matters are on your mind, and your interest in the topic.

Even 15% of the original information may seem to be a very small amount but the percentage can be dramatically increased by revising the original text after one week, and then again after two weeks. By this time, the facts will now be retained by your so-called long-term memory store and up to 80% of the original material will be recalled in this way.

Bearing in mind that the time each student can maintain concentration will vary considerably, there are certain revision principles which can be followed:

❶ Make a **realistic** estimate of how much you can revise each week over a period beginning perhaps three months before your examination.

❷ Divide your revision time into 30-minute periods separated by intervals of about 10 minutes.

❸ Monitor your progress and adjust your weekly targets accordingly.

DIFFERENT TYPES OF EXAMINATION QUESTION

Structured questions

These are the most common questions used at GCSE level in biology. The questions are divided into parts (a), (b), (c), etc, and the parts are often subdivided into (i), (ii), etc. There is a structure built into each question which can usually be recognized as beginning with the easiest parts and becoming progressively demanding towards the end.

For each part of the question there are a number of lines or a space for your answer. This is a guide to the amount of detail required for the answer. If you should need more space, continue your answer on a separate piece of paper which will be supplied on request. Remember to label any extra paper with the correct question number.

For each part of the question, the number of marks available is shown in brackets e.g. (3). If a part is worth three marks, the answer needs to be more than one or two words. You would usually be expected to write three points to gain three marks.

To give you a guide as you work through structured questions, the papers are usually designed to enable you to score one mark per minute. A question worth 5 marks should therefore take about five minutes to answer.

Questions are designed to assess more skills than just recall, including:

(a) using **symbolic representations** – testing the skill of the student to understand and use graphical information and models of biological information;

(b) using **observation** – testing the ability to decide the relevant features of a problem and using observed patterns to make predictions;

(c) **interpretation and application** – where actual data is presented to the student to test the skill of producing hypotheses consistent with the data, and assessing the validity of such hypotheses.

Keep your answers as concise as possible. An examiner may not be able to see that you have the right idea of the answer if it is written in an overcomplicated way.

Introduction

Free-response questions

These can include essay questions. In this type of question, you are able to develop your answer in different ways. You can write as much as you wish. Candidates often do not write enough, or they 'pad out' their answer with irrelevant information. Remember, you can only score marks when your answer matches the marking points on the examiner's mark scheme.

In free-response questions it is important to plan your answer before starting it, allocating the correct amount of time to each part of the question. Attention to spelling, punctuation and grammar is important and is worth up to 5% extra. These marks are gained especially for the correct use and spelling of technical terms. This is something you should check at the end of the examination if you have time to spare.

Sample question

Name one form of atmospheric pollution. State its source and explain its effects on the environment. (6)

Suggest ways of reducing this form of pollution. (2)

This question should take about eight to ten minutes to answer. You need to choose a form of atmospheric pollution of which you have detailed knowledge.

Plan

Nitrogen oxides and acid rain would be a good choice.

- State the form of pollution and its source.
- Explain how these chemicals react in the atmosphere to form acid rain.
- Explain the effects of acid rain on living organisms and buildings.
- State ways of reducing this pollution.

Here is a sample answer.

Oxides of nitrogen, NO and NO_2 (NO_x), enter the air from the exhausts of motor vehicles. *(1 mark for the name of the pollutant and 1 mark for its source)*

Nitrogen dioxide reacts with water vapour and oxygen in the air to form nitric acid. This becomes part of a cloud and eventually falls as acid rain or acid snow. *(1 mark for a description of how acid rain is formed)*

The acid rain reacts with minerals in the soil, making them soluble. These minerals are then leached from the topsoil and plants cannot obtain these nutrients. *(1 mark for the effect of acid rain on plants)*

The acidic water and certain metal ions which leach from the soil enter rivers and lakes. Fish suffer because the effects of excess acidity prevent their eggs hatching and also interfere with gaseous exchange at the gills. *(1 mark for the effect of acid rain on fish)*

Acid rain causes corrosion to stonework by dissolving limestone. *(1 mark for the effect of acid rain on buildings)*

Lime (calcium hydroxide) can be added to lakes to neutralize some of the acid. Pollution by nitrogen oxides is reduced when catalytic converters are fitted to vehicle exhausts. These cause the exhaust fumes to break down into nitrogen, water and carbon dioxide. Nitrogen is present in the atmosphere and is not a pollutant. *(2 marks for suggesting ways to reduce pollution)*

Introduction

TERMS USED IN QUESTIONS

Sometimes candidates find difficulty in understanding the meaning of instructions given in questions. The following table contains a list of common terms which often introduce questions on examination papers, together with an explanation of each.

Instruction in question	Meaning
Describe	Extended prose, merely stating observations
Give an account of	Write an explanatory description
Discuss	Give an account of the various views on a topic
Compare	Put side by side, one or more similarities
Contrast	Put side by side, one or more differences
Distinguish between	A combination of 'compare' and 'contrast'
Explain/Account for	Extended prose, giving reasons for observations
State	A brief statement with no supporting evidence
Define	State precisely and concisely what is meant
Suggest	Give examples or explanations where there may be more than one correct answer. You could apply your answer to a situation outside the syllabus
Summarize	Give a brief account of
Survey/Outline	Give a general (as opposed to detailed) account of
Comment on	Make explanatory remarks or criticisms on
Illustrate by reference to	Use named examples to demonstrate the idea or principle

Introduction

ASSESSMENT OBJECTIVES IN BIOLOGY

Assessment Objectives are the intellectual and practical skills you should be able to show. Opportunities must be made by the Examiner when setting the examination paper for you to demonstrate your mastery of these skills when you answer the question paper.

Traditionally the Assessment Objective of knowledge and understanding has been regarded as the most important skill to develop. Candidates have been directed to learn large bodies of knowledge to recall in the examination. Whilst not wanting in any way to devalue the learning of facts, it should be remembered that on modern papers knowledge and understanding can only contribute about half of the marks available. The other half of the marks are acquired by mastery of the other Assessment Objectives, namely:

- Communicate scientific observations, ideas and arguments effectively.
- Select and use reference materials and translate data from one form to another.
- Interpret, evaluate and make informed judgements from relevant facts, observations and phenomena.
- Solve qualitative and quantitative problems.

1 Communicate scientific observations, ideas and arguments effectively
(*weighting on papers approximately 5–10%*)

In any examination, communication of information to the examiner is of primary importance. This Assessment Objective should not be confused with spelling, punctuation and grammar (SPAG) — up to 5% added to your mark on the paper for the quality of your spelling, punctuation and grammar.

Questions are built into the paper to test you ability to communicate scientific information. Often these questions require extended answers.

In this type of question it is important to look at your answer objectively after you have written it and try to judge whether your answer is communicating information effectively.

2 Select and use reference materials and translate data from one form to another (*weighting on papers approximately 10–15%*)

In questions testing this Assessment Objective you are asked frequently to pick information from a chart or table and use it in another form, e.g. to draw a graph, a pie chart, bar chart, etc. You may be asked to complete a table using information from a graph.

It is important to transfer the skills you have acquired in Mathematics to your work in Biology.

Skill acquired	Approx. grade in GCSE Maths
Read information from graphs or simple diagrams	F
Work out simple percentages	F
Construct and use pie charts	F
Use graphs	E
Plot graphs from data provided. The axes and scales are given to you.	E
Be able to draw the best line through points on a graph	C
Select the most appropriate axes and scales for graph plotting	B

It is reasonable, therefore, to conclude that at Higher level you might be required to use a blank piece of graph paper and choose your own scales and axes. Then you would plot the points and draw a line of best fit through the points. If you are doing this, remember:

Introduction

❶ To draw your graph as large as possible on the graph paper by choosing scales appropriately. Avoid choosing scales where, for example, 3 small squares are equivalent to 5°C. It would be better if 1 small square was equivalent to 1°C or 2 °C. With this type of graph drawing, marks are usually awarded for the choice of scales and for labelled axes.

❷ To plot each point with a dot or small cross. Circle the dot or cross to make its position clear.

❸ Your line of best fit, whether it is a straight line or a curve, does not have to go through all the points. Some points may not be in the correct place, even if you plotted them correctly, because of inaccuracies in the experiment or experimental error.

On a Central tier paper a similar graph may have to be drawn but it would be more appropriate for the examiner to provide a grid with axes and scales given. Then you would only have to plot the points and draw the line of best fit. It would probably be worth fewer marks than a graph on the Higher tier paper.

3 Interpret, evaluate and make informed judgements from relevant facts, observations and phenomena (*weighting on papers approximately 10–15%*)

Questions testing this Assessment Objective are often difficult for candidates. It is much easier to test this on a Higher tier paper than on a Basic tier paper.

The command word 'suggest' is very frequently used as the information given, perhaps in a paragraph, table, diagram or any combination of these, is open to more than one interpretation.

Look carefully at all of the information given and look for possible alternative interpretations before writing your answer.

4 Solve qualitative and quantitative problems (*weighting on papers approximately 10–15%*)

Again opportunities to test this Assessment Objective are greater, especially for solving quantitative problems, on Higher tier papers.

Qualitative problems can include describing the effects of humans on the environment or applications of Biology. Quantitative problems include genetics and ecological energy transfer. Remember, when attempting to carry out a calculation, to:

❶ Use all of the information given to you. If the question gives energy values, they should be used.

❷ Show all of your working so credit can be given if you do not get the correct answer but get some way through the question.

❸ Give correct units to your answers if there are units.

You will see questions throughout this book where the question is designed to test Assessment Objectives other than knowledge and understanding.

Life processes 1

REVISION SUMMARY

Energy and life

Plants and some bacteria are the only organisms that can make food. Animals either eat plants or they eat other animals which themselves have eaten plants.

The process by which plants make food is called **photosynthesis.** Plants use inorganic materials, in particular *carbon dioxide* from the atmosphere and *water* from the soil, and in the presence of *chlorophyll* and *energy* (in the form of sunlight) they manufacture *carbohydrates*.

Photosynthesis can be divided into two basic stages:

❶ *Splitting water* using energy from the sun.

❷ *Reduction of carbon dioxide* by the addition of hydrogen.

Stage 1

Energy from sunlight, trapped by the green pigment *chlorophyll*, splits water molecules into oxygen and hydrogen, the process of **photolysis**.

$$4H_2O \xrightarrow[\text{Chlorophyll}]{\text{Sunlight}} 4[OH] + 4[H]$$

$$4[OH] \longrightarrow 2H_2O + O_2 \text{ (by-products)}$$

Stage 2

The hydrogen is combined with carbon dioxide in a complex series of reduction reactions. The product acts as a starting point for the manufacture of most carbohydrates, proteins, fats and most vitamins. The significance of photosynthesis to animals is thus:

- It provides the source of their dietary requirements.
- It provides them with oxygen (given off in Stage 1).
- It uses the carbon dioxide that they produce as waste during respiration.

Respiration is the release of *energy* from *glucose* and occurs in all living cells.

$$\underset{\text{Glucose}}{C_6H_{12}O_6} + \underset{\text{Oxygen}}{6O_2} \xrightarrow{\text{Enzymes}} \underset{\text{Carbon dioxide}}{6CO_2} + \underset{\text{Water}}{6H_2O} + \underset{\text{ATP}}{\text{Energy}}$$

The equation is a gross over-simplification of the process because:

❶ Many other intermediate enzyme-controlled reactions occur.

❷ Most of the oxidation takes place by the action of hydrogen carriers removing hydrogen from the glucose, then oxygen is added during the final stage only.

❸ Energy is liberated in a succession of stages, a small amount at a time.

❹ The energy is in *adenosine triphosphate* (ATP), which acts as an energy carrier. ATP carries energy to the cell, then releases the energy. During this release of energy, ATP loses one of its phosphate groups to become *adenosine diphosphate* (ADP).

Respiration and gaseous exchange

Respiration is the chemical process which releases *energy* from *glucose* in every living cell during oxidation.

In mammals, gaseous exchange takes place between the lungs and the blood. This is made possible by breathing. In simple animals, individual cells are in direct contact with the environment. The more complex forms have blood to transport materials.

Atmospheric pressure and concentration of gases in the air both play important roles in the diffusion of gases through membranes. Another vital property of gases is the ability to dissolve in water. Oxygen, in the alveoli of the lungs, diffuses into the blood stream.

Metabolism involves respiration and the growth process. The rate at which it occurs during rest is called the basal metabolic rate.

1 Life processes

REVISION SUMMARY

Since oxygen is needed for the complete oxidation of glucose, this type of respiration is called **aerobic respiration**. Sometimes respiration takes place without the use of oxygen. This process is called **anaerobic respiration**. Yeast respires anaerobically by converting glucose into ethanol.

$$\text{Glucose} \rightarrow \text{Ethanol} + \text{Carbon dioxide} + \text{Energy}$$

This is called alcoholic fermentation.

During strenuous exercise, we are unable to breathe fast enough for oxygen to be supplied to our muscles. Our muscles obtain energy from anaerobic respiration. In this process, *lactic acid* is formed.

$$\text{Glucose} \rightarrow \text{Lactic acid} + \text{Energy}$$

Lactic acid is a mild poison and causes muscles to ache. When the exercise is finished, oxygen is needed to break down the lactic acid into carbon dioxide and water. The oxygen needed to break down lactic acid is called the **oxygen debt**. Alcoholic fermentation and anaerobic respiration produce less energy than aerobic respiration.

Excretion

Various wastes result from protein metabolism. They are removed from the body through *kidneys*, *skin*, and *lungs*. The kidneys are the body's most important excretory organs. They filter practically all the nitrogenous wastes from blood. The skin also excretes wastes. It gets rid of water, salts, and some urea in sweat. In addition, sweat helps control your body temperature.

Response and movement

The **central nervous system** is composed of the *brain* and the *spinal cord*. They communicate with all parts of the body via nerves.

There are three types of nerve cells or neurones.

❶ *Sensory neurones* which carry messages from the *receptors* (sense organs) to the spinal cord and brain (the central nervous system).

❷ *Effector neurones* (motor neurones) carry messages from the central nervous system (CNS) to the *effectors* (muscles or glands).

❸ *Connector neurones* (relay neurones) carry messages through the CNS between the sensory neurones and effector neurones.

Sense organ	Stimulus it is sensitive to
Skin	touch, pressure, pain, heat, cold
Eye	light
Ear	vibrations
Nose	chemicals in solution
Tongue	chemicals in solution

Movement in humans is brought about by *antagonistic pairs* of muscles acting across joints and pulling on bones which act as levers.

The control of the muscles is by conscious effort, when it is *voluntary*, and involves the central nervous system. However, there are also rapid, *reflex*, protective actions which involve movement but do *not* require conscious effort. The following table gives some examples of reflex actions.

8

Life processes 1

REVISION SUMMARY

Reflex	Stimulus	Response
Coughing	Irritant in the throat	Contraction of abdominal muscles and expiratory intercostal muscles; relaxation of the diaphragm
Swallowing	Food at the back of the throat	Soft palate is raised; epiglottis is closed; peristalsis takes place
Blinking	Object coming towards the eye	Contraction of eyelid muscles
Knee-jerk	Pressure/pain on knee	Contraction of flexor muscles
Pupil contraction/dilation	Change in light intensity	Contraction of muscles of the iris

Drugs and the nervous system

Tobacco is not addictive in the sense that narcotic drugs are. However, it does pose serious health problems, as it tends to shorten life and seems to contribute to many diseases.

Alcohol is a depressant. Used excessively, it leads to alcoholism. Alcohol can cause organic diseases which may be fatal. It can be antisocial and is dangerous when used by people who drive.

Misuse of **drugs** can be harmful to the users and may even cause death. Drug addiction can be a psychological problem, a physical one, or both. *Narcotic drugs* can become physically addictive. People who take them habitually often do so in order to escape from problems. This is psychological addiction. But as the body builds up a drug tolerance, so addicts must take more and more in order to 'escape'. Physically, the body demands more in order to avoid painful *withdrawal symptoms*. Narcotics are illegal, with just a few available on prescription. Consequently, many addicts spend much of their time looking for ways to obtain drugs and invariably turn to crime, which creates problems for both them and society in general.

Chemical control

Ductless glands are called **endocrine glands**. They secrete *hormones* directly into the blood stream.

Glands are controlled by their influence on each other, by feedback, and by the nervous system. Their delicate balance is maintained by *homeostatic mechanisms*. If any one of the endocrine glands slows down or becomes overactive, the chemical balance is upset and the body reacts, making the person feel ill.

If you need to revise this subject more thoroughly, see the relevant topics in the *Letts* GCSE *Biology* and *Human Biology Study Guides*.

1 Life processes

QUESTIONS

1 The diagram shows the alimentary canal.

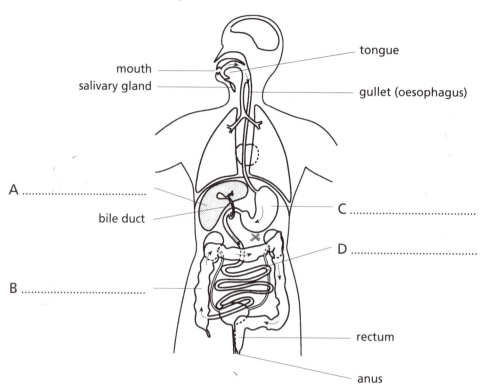

(a) (i) Label the diagram choosing your answers from this list.

   gall bladder   large intestine   liver

   small intestine spleen   stomach   (4)

   (ii) The pancreas is missing from the diagram.
         On the diagram mark with an X where the pancreas should be. (1)

   (iii) State what is secreted by the pancreas.

   The pancreas gives out insulin

   .... (2)

(b) Draw a line to match the word with its description.
    The first one has been done for you.

   enzyme   the process which changes insoluble food into
                     soluble substances

   gastric juice   a biological catalyst

   peristalsis   fluid made in the liver, stored in the gall bladder

   bile   a wave of muscular contraction

                     fluid containing enzymes and hydrochloric acid   (3)

Life processes 1

(c) A disease in cows causes the inner wall of the small intestine to become smooth and flat. Infected cows rapidly lose weight and usually die.

Suggest why this change to the intestine wall causes the cows to die.

....

....

....

.... (4)

(d)

> **Wholemeal Bread is Good For You**
>
> EAT SOME FIBRE EVERYDAY
> AND
> KEEP THE DOCTOR AWAY!

This advertisement offers some good advice.
Explain why fibre is needed in our diet.

....

....

....

.... (3)

2   The enzyme amylase breaks down starch to maltose.
    The effect of temperature on this action of amylase was investigated. The results are recorded below.

TUBE A
Starch suspension and amylase kept at 10 °C.

time (minutes)	0	1	2	3	4	5	6	7	8	9	10
amount of starch in tube (mg)	10	9.9	9.5	9.2	9	8.8	8.5	8.2	8	7.5	7

Life processes

QUESTIONS

TUBE B
Starch suspension and amylase kept at 20 °C.

time (minutes)	0	1	2	3	4	5	6	7	8	9	10
amount of starch in tube (mg)	10	9.8	9.2	8.5	8	7	6.2	7	5.2	4.8	4

TUBE C
Starch suspension and amylase kept at 40 °C

time (minutes)	0	1	2	3	4	5	6	7	8	9	10
amount of starch in tube (mg)	10	9.5	8	7	5	3.5	1	0.4	0.2	0	0

TUBE D
Starch suspension and **boiled** amylase kept at 40 °C

time (minutes)	0	1	2	3	4	5	6	7	8	9	10
amount of starch in tube (mg)	10	10	10	10	10	10	10	10	10	10	10

(a) (i) Complete the graph by plotting the results for tube B. (3)

(ii) Finish the graph by drawing the best line for tube B. (2)

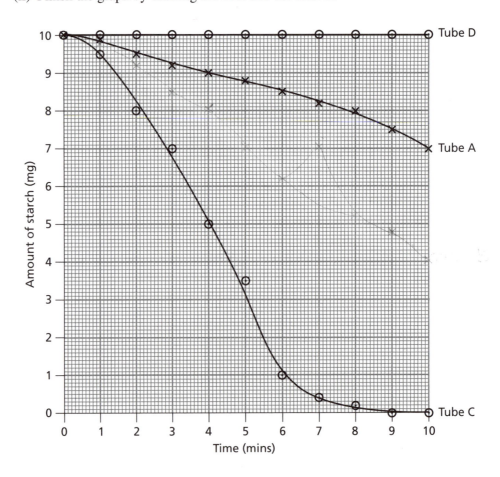

12

Life processes 1

QUESTIONS

Use the graph to help you answer the following questions.

(b) (i) At what temperature did the enzyme work the fastest?

.... (1)

(ii) When the enzyme was kept at 40 °C and had **not** been boiled, how long did it take the enzyme to break down the starch?

.... (1)

(iii) What two substances were left in tube C at the end of the experiment?

1. ....

2. .... (2)

(c) Describe the effect a high temperature has on the enzyme amylase.

....

.... (2)

(d) Biological washing powders contain protein-digesting enzymes. Suggest the advice you would give to the consumer on how to obtain the best results from a biological washing powder. Back up your advice with scientific evidence.

....

....

....

.... (3)

3   The diagram shows a vertical section through a leaf.

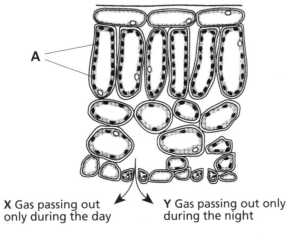

X Gas passing out only during the day   Y Gas passing out only during the night

13

1 Life processes

QUESTIONS

(a) (i) State the function of parts A.

.... (1)

(ii) Name the gases represented by

X ....

Y .... (2)

(b)

Diagrams are drawn to the same scale.
Amount of light received (arbitrary units)

5   10   15   20

The drawings show the average size of leaves from the same plant. All the leaves were of the same age but had been exposed to different light intensities because some grew in shadier conditions than others. Explain these observations.

....

....

....

.... (2)

(c) The following diagram shows part of a microscopic section of a lung.

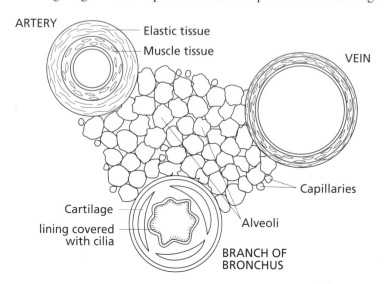

Life processes 1

QUESTIONS

State two features shared by leaves and human lungs that make them efficient gas exchange surfaces.

(i) ....

(ii) .... (2)

(d) State two ways in which leaves and lungs differ as gas exchange surfaces.

(i) ....

....

(ii) ....

.... (2)

4 (a) The diagram below shows an elbow joint.

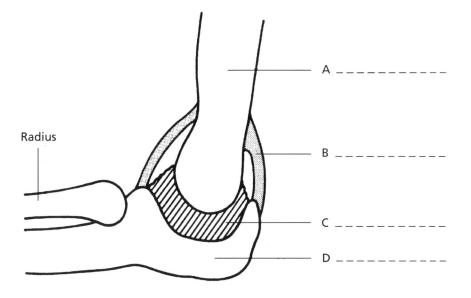

(i) Label parts A–D. (2)

(ii) State the function of part B. (1)

(iii) On the diagram, draw and label the cartilage in the correct position. (2)

(iv) Describe two features of the joint which help it move smoothly.

....

.... (2)

1 Life processes

QUESTIONS

(v) Explain how the action of pairs of muscles causes the bones to move at the joint.

....

.... (2)

(b) When a joint is damaged, medical technology can be applied by fitting an artificial joint as shown in the diagram.

Give three visible differences between the normal joint and the artificial metal joint.

....

....

.... (3)

5   The liver is an organ of homeostasis.

(a) What is meant by the term homeostasis?

....

.... (1)

(b) Name one substance found in the blood which is regulated by the liver.

.... (1)

(c) Name two hormones, produced by the pancreas, involved in homeostasis.

(i) ....

(ii) .... (2)

Life processes 1

QUESTIONS

(d) Explain the function of each hormone.

(i) Hormone 1 ....

....

....

.... (2)

(ii) Hormone 2 ....

....

....

.... (2)

(e) The normal concentration of glucose in the blood is 0.1 g per 100 cm³.
Why is it dangerous for the concentration of glucose to drop below this level?

....

....

.... (1)

(f) The following flow diagram demonstrates the principle of negative feedback to maintain the balance of materials in the body.

```
            causes ──► A INCREASED STIMULUS ──── causes ──►
                                                              
 D DECREASED RESPONSE                              B INCREASED RESPONSE
                                                              
            causes ──── C DECREASED STIMULUS ◄──── causes
```

Complete the following flow diagram to show how the production of a hormone by the pancreas demonstrates negative feedback. Fill in the blanks A – D.

```
                    A ........................
         causes ──►                          
                     ........................    causes ──►
                                                            
 D ........................                        B ........................
   ........................                        release from the pancreas
                                                            
         causes ──── Decrease in concentration of ◄──── causes
                    C ........................
```
(4)

17

1 Life processes

QUESTIONS

6 The diagram represents part of the digestive system of a human.

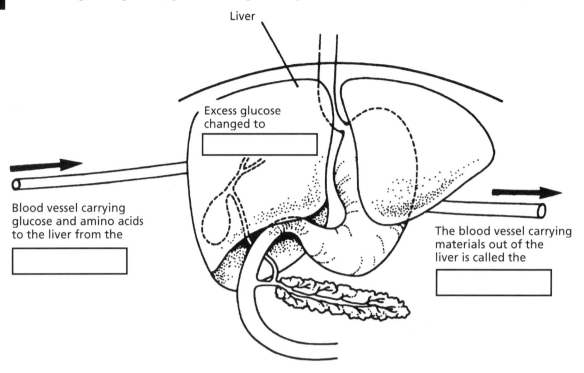

(a) (i) On the diagram, label with an X, the connection of the pancreas to the alimentary canal. (1)

(ii) Complete the diagram by writing in the boxes the correct words selected from the list below.

hepatic artery, hepatic vein, glycogen, sugar, urine, urea, ileum, pancreas. (3)

(b) Complete the table below to show the chemical elements present in the foods listed. The first one has been done for you.

Class of food	Chemical elements present
Carbohydrate	Carbon, hydrogen, oxygen
Protein	
Fat	

(2)

(c) Underline the correct answer below. Digestive enzymes are essential because they

(i) are protein;

(ii) are unchanged after a reaction;

(iii) can help break down large molecules;

(iv) are denatured by high temperatures. (1)

Life processes 1

QUESTIONS

(d) If the normal body temperature is 37 °C, which of the following graphs is correct for enzyme activity in the human body?

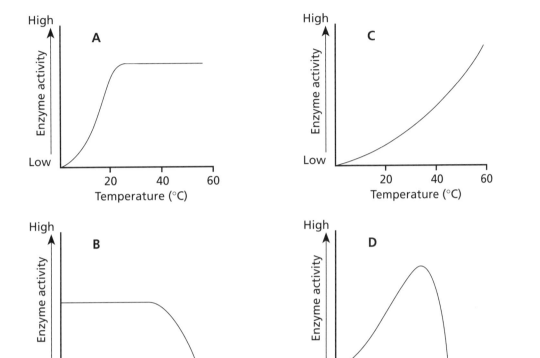

(1)

7 There is evidence to suggest that a high cholesterol level in the blood is linked to diet.

Graph A shows the relationship between death rate and cholesterol levels in the blood of people in the USA.

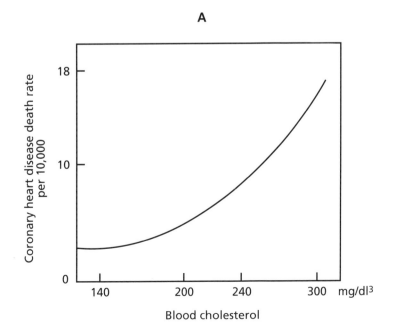

19

1 Life processes

QUESTIONS

(a) What can you conclude from Graph A?

....

.... (1)

(b) Graph B shows the amount of cholesterol in the blood of Americans aged between 20 years and 74 years.

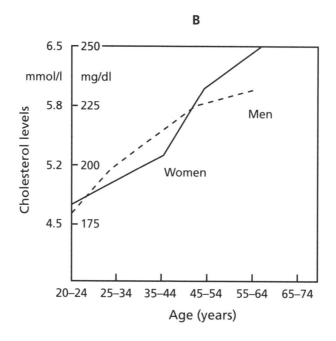

Use graph B and the given information to answer the question which follows. Substances called Low Density Lipoproteins (LDLs) carry cholesterol in the blood and release it on the inside of arteries. High Density Lipoproteins (HDLs) take cholesterol out of the blood and away from the walls of arteries.

A female sex hormone (oestrogen) reduces levels of LDLs in the blood and increases HDLs. On average, females stop producing oestrogen between the ages of 50 and 60. Explain, fully, the health risk from heart disease in these women.

....

....

....

....

.... (4)

(c) Name two factors, other than diet, which may lead to heart disease.

....

.... (2)

8 (a) Use the table below and your knowledge to answer the questions which follow.
The table shows the composition of four body fluids associated with kidney function.

Substance or cell	Body fluid P	Body fluid W	Body fluid Y	Body fluid Z	Dialysis fluid
Salts	+	+	+	+	
Urea	+	+	+		
Glucose	+	+		+	
Proteins		+		+	
Water	+	+	+	+	+
Blood cells		+		+	

+ = present

In a healthy person, which of the columns could represent the contents of

(i) the bladder ....

(ii) the artery supplying the kidney ....

(iii) the vein taking blood from the kidney .... (3)

(b) The diagram shows the principle of a kidney machine.

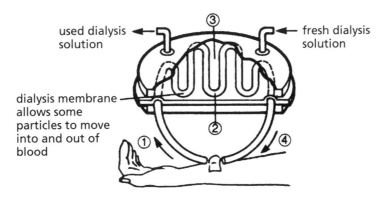

1 – a tube connects a person's vein to the dialysis machine.
2 – inside the machine, blood is pumped across one side of dialysing membranes.
3 – dialysis solution is on the other side of the dialysing membrane, kept fresh by a constant flow.
4 – blood returns to the person's arm.

1 Life processes

QUESTIONS

By adding two (+) symbols in the dialysis fluid column in the table, show the composition of the dialysing fluid to be used so that valuable substances are not lost from the body. (2)

(c) The following apparatus can be used to demonstrate dialysis.

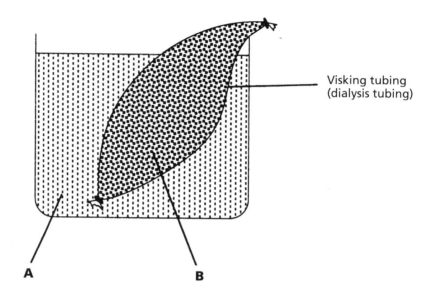

Visking tubing (dialysis tubing)

A   B

Choose columns from the table to represent fluids A and B.

A: ....

B: .... (2)

(d) State one advantage and one disadvantage of a kidney transplant compared to the use of a kidney machine for a person with kidney failure.

(i) One advantage.

.... (1)

(ii) One disadvantage.

.... (1)

Inheritance and evolution 2

REVISION SUMMARY

Cell growth and reproduction

Organisms grow by the division called **mitosis**.

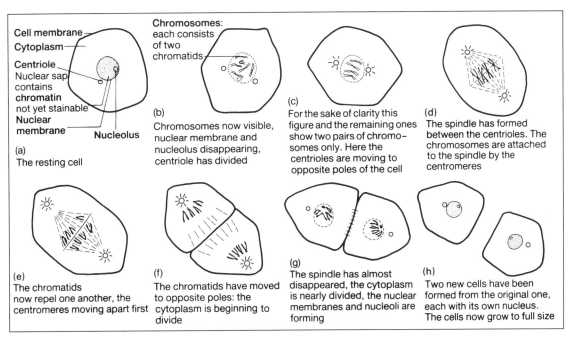

Stages in mitosis

Each daughter cell produced in mitosis has the *diploid chromosome number*. Further, the chromosomes of the daughter cells are identical to those of the mother cell. All body cells in all members of the same species contain the same kind and number of chromosomes.

Sperms and eggs are produced by a different kind of division, known as **meiosis**.

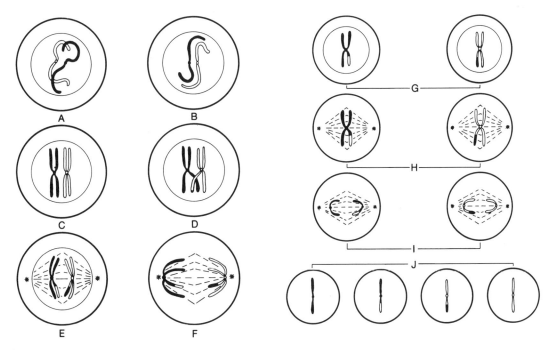

Key: Maternal chromosone is white
Paternal chromosone is black; Diploid number = 2

Meiosis in a gamete-forming cell

2 Inheritance and evolution

REVISION SUMMARY

The stages in meiosis, as shown in the previous diagram, are as follows:

❶ Each *chromosome* moves towards, and begins to pair with, its partner. The pairing process results in a very *close contact* along the whole of the length of the chromosomes (B). Thus the first stage of *meiosis* differs from that in mitosis. At the start of mitosis the chromosomes consist of two chromatids which are formed by duplication, but in meiosis whole *pairs* of chromosomes come together.

❷ While in this close union, the chromosomes shorten and thicken, and each becomes *duplicated* into **two chromatids** (C). At this stage the *nuclear membrane* begins to disintegrate.

❸ Along the length of the pairs of chromosomes, individual **chromatids cross** one another in complex ways. As a result of this, chromatids **exchange** various sections (D). The force of attraction that up to this point has held the pairs of chromosomes together now ceases to operate fully, and the pairs of chromosomes begin to *separate* (E). (In the diagram for simplicity only one cross-over is shown.)

❹ The chromosomes separate completely and move to *opposite* poles of the cell (F). The *cytoplasm divides* (G). At this point, each daughter cell still has the *diploid* number of chromosomes, but because of *crossing over* of sections of the chromatids, **genes** from one partner have been mixed with genes from the other partner.

❺ Each new cell undergoes a *mitotic* division. The chromosomes, each consisting of *two complete chromatids* (even though parts have been exchanged), line up along the centre of the new cell (H). One set of chromatids passes to each pole of the cell. Each new set of chromosomes starts to form a nucleus (I).

❻ A division of the cytoplasm occurs and nuclear membranes re-appear. As a result, **four gametes**, each with the *haploid* number of chromosomes, have been formed from an original *diploid* cell (J).

The *significance* of meiosis is:
(a) The formation of cells with **half** the normal number of chromosomes.
(b) **Mixing of genes** between pairs of chromosomes contributing to **variation** within the chromosomes.

Meiosis involves two stages of division. The cells that result contain the *haploid chromosome number*. When these cells join in fertilization, the diploid number is restored.

Principles of heredity

It was the work of Gregor Mendel (1822–1884) with garden peas that opened up the field of **heredity** to science. Mendel's hypotheses about **genes**, which he called factors, have become basic principles of **genetics**. Among these principles are the ideas that genes:

- control heredity,
- occur in pairs, and
- may be *dominant* or *recessive*.

The genetic material

Many years have passed since Gregor Mendel's experiments with garden peas opened up the science of genetics. Since 1900, scientists have probed deeper and deeper into the mysteries of the living cell and its genetic material. Most of the traits we inherit are necessary and helpful. Some are harmful. We are finding out more and more about these genetic problems. Often, learning the cause of a problem leads to its correction. We are beginning to learn the effects of genes on such things as cystic fibrosis, Huntington's chorea, haemophilia and many other conditions.

Genes sometimes *mutate* and a major cause of mutations is high energy radiation. Radiation from artifical sources and natural sources will cause changes in the structure of genes, leading to mutation.

24

Inheritance and evolution

Applied genetics

For many centuries, people have worked at breeding improved strains of plants and animals. Three important methods of breeding are **mass selection**, **hybridization**, and **inbreeding**. Mass selection involves choosing the parents for further breeding from a large number of individuals. Hybridization is the crossing of two different strains. An example of inbreeding is self pollination in plants. Over several generations, the offspring with the desired traits are sorted out by mass selection. In the end, a pure strain is produced.

Another form of applied genetics is **genetic engineering**. This relies on isolating a useful gene from one organism and putting it into another of a different species. For example, scientists often isolate genes from human chromosomes which control the production of certain hormones. They put these useful genes into bacteria or yeast cells. The human genes are transferred to the bacteria or yeast to increase production of the hormone. The microbes multiply very rapidly and can be cultured relatively cheaply. In fact they can provide almost unlimited amounts of substances that are practically unobtainable in bulk in any other way.

Evolution

Life on Earth probably began more than three thousand million years ago. In all the time since than, life has been in a constant state of change. New species develop; old ones change.

Biologists understand this process as **evolution by natural selection**, which was first suggested by Charles Darwin (1809–1882). New traits appear in organisms as a result of mutations or new gene combinations. Whether these traits are helpful or harmful depends on the environment. All organisms face a constant struggle for survival (survival of the fittest to breed). Those with helpful traits are more likely to survive and pass the traits on. Organisms without these traits tend to die out. In the end, all members of a population may have the helpful traits.

REVISION SUMMARY

If you need to revise this subject more thoroughly, see the relevant topics in the *Letts GCSE Biology* and *Human Biology Study Guides*.

2 Inheritance and evolution

QUESTIONS

1 In 1966 a Canadian cat breeder noticed that a hairless kitten was born in a litter of kittens from normal parents. The cat breeder used some of the cats from this family to select a new *hairless* breed which she called Sphinx.

(a) Assume that the gene for *hairless* is recessive to the gene for hairy, H.
Describe how the cat breeder would breed large numbers of Sphinx cats from the original parents and further matings. The gene for *hairless* is not sex linked.

KEY .... (1)

Parental genotypes .... (1)

First Cross

(1)

Second Cross

(1)

(b) Write the genotypes of three sets of parents which could never produce hairless cats unless a mutation takes place.

(i) .... × ....

(ii) .... × ....

(iii) .... × .... (3)

(c) The sex of cats is determined in the same way as the sex of all other mammals. Show, in the box below, how the chance of producing male or female kittens is 50%.

KEY: The sex chromosomes of the male kitten are ....

The sex chromosomes of the female kitten are .... (1)

(1)

Inheritance and evolution 2

QUESTIONS

2 Scientists have found that they can produce animals with identical genes by cloning. One way to do this is to remove the nucleus from an unfertilized egg cell and replace it with a nucleus from a body cell. The egg cell with its new nucleus can then grow into a new individual.

(a) State the main difference in the amount of genetic material between the nucleus which has been removed and the one which has replaced it.

....

....

.... (3)

(b) Early cloning experiments were done on the eggs of frogs and toads. This was done because it was easier than using eggs from mammals. Suggest and explain one reason why this was easier.

....

.... (2)

(c) More recent experiments have been done by removing the nucleus from an egg cell of a rabbit. A liver cell from another rabbit was used to provide a nucleus which was then placed into the egg. The following diagram shows the main stages in the process.

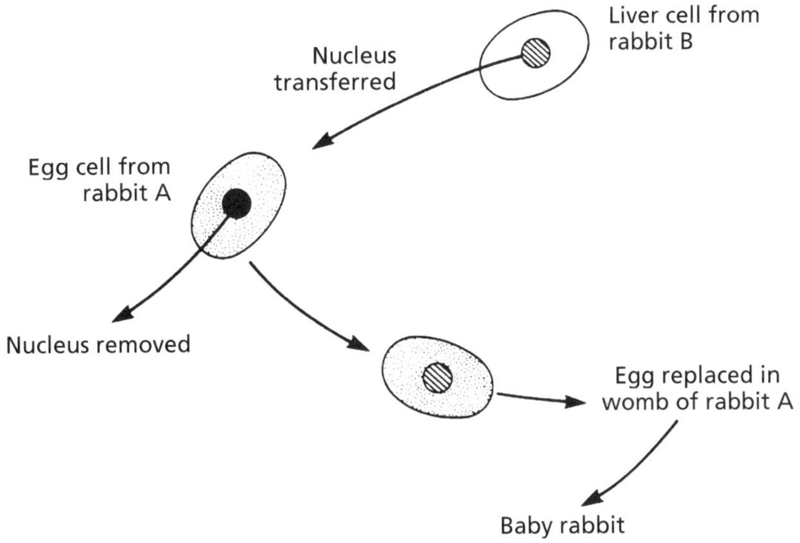

(i) Which rabbit, A or B, will the baby rabbit look like? .... (1)

(ii) Explain your answer.

....

.... (2)

2 Inheritance and evolution

QUESTIONS

(d) Cloning can be used with many different animals. For example, cloning could be used to improve the quality of sheep. The following diagram shows the main stages in the process. Fill in the four boxes to briefly describe stages 2, 3, 4 and 5.

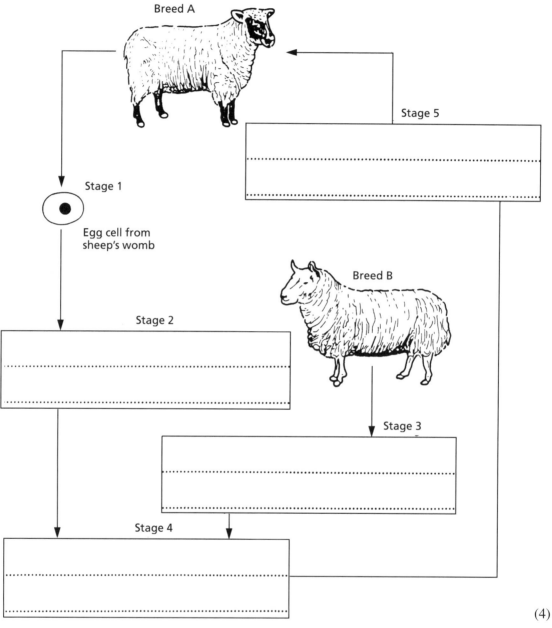

(4)

(e) Suggest one advantage and one disadvantage of the cloning of farm animals. Give your reasons.

Advantage ....

.... (1)

Reason ....

.... (1)

Inheritance and evolution

Disadvantage ....

.... (1)

Reason ....

.... (1)

(f) Cloning is a fairly new way of changing the features of living things. However, changes have been taking place amongst living things on Earth for millions of years due to another process.

(i) What is this process called? .... (1)

(ii) Explain how this process may have caused giraffes to change from a short-necked species to a long-necked species.

....

....

....

....

....

.... (6)

SEG 1993

3 (a) Haemophilia is a genetic disorder in which people cannot produce a blood-clotting factor. Sufferers have difficulty in stopping bleeding. The development of an industrial process for the production of blood-clotting factor would involve the following steps.

Steps

A Extracting and purifying the clotting factor
B Inserting the gene into the genetic material of the bacteria
C Identifying the human gene responsible for production of the clotting factor
D Isolating the gene which controls production of the clotting factor
E Growing large numbers of genetically engineered bacteria

Use the letters to show the correct order in which the steps would occur.

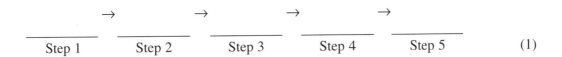

Step 1   Step 2   Step 3   Step 4   Step 5   (1)

2 Inheritance and evolution

QUESTIONS

(b) State **two** advantages which result from the use of genetically engineered bacteria in production processes.

1. ....

....

2. ....

.... (1)

SEB 1994

4 Sometimes an organism shows a new characteristic as a result of mutation, which it then passes on to its offspring.

(a) In which type of cell must this mutation have occurred?

.... (1)

(b) Explain how natural selection may cause the mutation to become common several generations later.

....

....

.... (3)

5

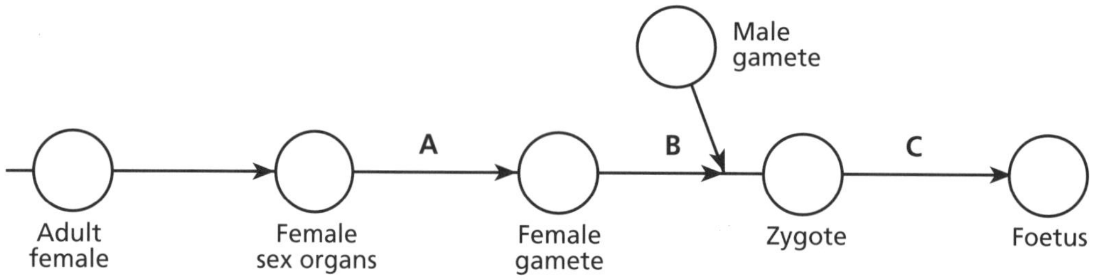

Adult female → Female sex organs —A→ Female gamete —B→ Zygote —C→ Foetus
(Male gamete arrow into Zygote)

(a) If the correct number of chromosomes for an adult male is 46, put the correct number in each circle on the diagram above. (2)

(b) Name the types of cell division occurring at

(i) A...............................

(ii) C...............................

(iii) Name the process occurring at B...................... (3)

(c) (i) Mark with an X the point at which ovulation occurs. (1)

(ii) Mark with a Z a point at which implantation occurs. (1)

Populations and human influences 3

REVISION SUMMARY

Many people used to take **natural resources** for granted. We have wasted many of these resources and caused thousands of hectares of land to become useless.

- An increase in population has caused mass property development and a need to increase crop yields.
- The increased use of fertilizers, pesticides, silage, etc has had an adverse effect on the environment, often because the chemicals involved in these treatments find their way into water.
- Over-use of land has caused *soil erosion*.
- An increase of industry and transport has increased *air pollution*: e.g. emissions of sulphur dioxide and oxides of nitrogen cause acid rain; carbon dioxide causes the *Greenhouse Effect* and CFCs damage the ozone layer.

Large numbers of people, as well as industry, cause pollution problems. **Pollution** can be defined as anything which, when added to the environment, destroys its purity.

- **Biodegradable substances** are broken down by *bacteria*. This releases minerals for *recycling*. However, there is a limit as to how much can be taken care of in this way.
- Non-biodegradable substances are not broken down. In fact, they may be toxic to organisms in the environment.
- Air can be polluted by many chemicals, some of which are poisonous to plants and animals.
- Radioactive particles can cause tissue damage and death. It is most important that people realize the effects of human action and do something about them.

The population of the world as a whole has been *growing steadily*, though in individual countries there have been *fluctuations* in population size as people have migrated to newly discovered territories or have gone off in search of new food and mineral sources. Malthus, in 1798, suggested that because the population *increases faster* than food production there should be some sort of **birth control**. The growth of the world's population is now much faster than it has been in the past for the following reasons:

❶ The **increased effectiveness of medical science in saving lives** and virtually wiping out many formerly fatal diseases, such as *diptheria* and *smallpox*.

❷ Practically all mothers and babies survive childbirth because of **improved pre- and post-natal medical care**.

❸ Increased lifespan in the Western industrial countries due to a **better diet** than that enjoyed by our ancestors.

❹ **Agricultural development**.

❺ **Industrial development** due to technological advances leading to greater potential for trade and greater affluence.

Two consequences of an increasing population growth rate are:

- **shortage of food**,
- **pollution**.

If you need to revise this subject more thoroughly, see the relevant topics in the *Letts* GCSE *Biology* and *Human Biology Study Guides*.

3 Populations and human influences

QUESTIONS

1 The histograms below show the population age structure of two countries, A and B.

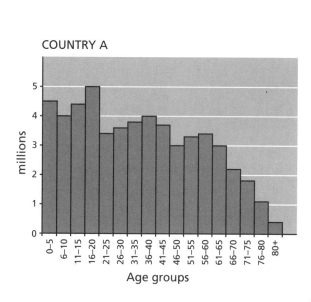
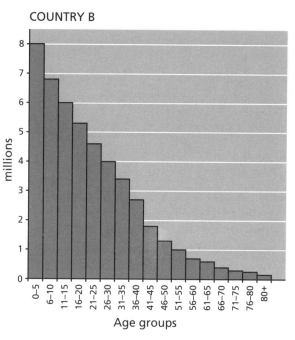

(a) If each year of the 0–5 age group contains the same number of children, calculate the birth rate in Country A.

    .... (1)

(b) Life expectancy may be measured by the age group containing 50% of the initial population. On this basis, what is the life expectancy of Country A?

    .... (1)

(c) The fertility rate of a population is the number of births per 1000 women of child bearing age per year. It is used for forecasting population trends and is calculated as follows:

$$\frac{\text{Number of births per year}}{\text{Number of women aged between 15 and 45}} \times 1000$$

What is the fertility rate for country A, assuming that half the population between 15 and 45 are women? Show your working.

(3)

(d) Country B is a poor country. State six ways in which bodies such as the World Health Organization (WHO) and the Food and Agriculture Organization (FAO) could improve standards of living and increase life expectancy.

    ....

    ....

Populations and human influences 3

QUESTIONS

....
....
....
.... (6)

2 The diagram shows some inputs into the Earth's atmosphere.

(a) (i) In which part of the atmosphere is the ozone layer situated?

.... (1)

(ii) Which gases reach the ozone layer?

.... (1)

(b) (i) Fill in the missing spaces using words from the box below.

| carbon dioxide | CFCs | oxygen | ozone | chlorine |

When some aerosols are used, ... are released into the
atmosphere. The action of sunlight on these gases changes them chemically,
releasing .... gas. This reacts with the ozone, producing
.... and chlorine monoxide. (3)

3 Populations and human influences

QUESTIONS

(ii) Describe and explain the likely effects on humans if this loss of ozone continues.

....

....

.... (2)

(c) State **two** ways in which the depletion of the ozone layer could be reduced.

1. ....

....

2. ....

.... (2)

NEAB 1993

3 On 26th April 1986, an accident at a nuclear power station at Chernobyl in Russia released large amounts of radioactive material into the atmosphere. The arrows on the map show the spread of radioactive material after the accident.

Populations and human influences 3

QUESTIONS

(a) (i) Suggest how radioactive material could have been spread from Chernobyl to Sweden within one day.

.... (1)

(ii) How might radioactive material high in the air have come down to the ground in Sweden?

.... (1)

(b) Laplanders in northern Sweden keep large herds of reindeer. These reindeer feed mainly on simple plants called lichens. By August 1986, many reindeer carcasses from slaughtered animals contained radioactive material at over ten times the Swedish legal limit and were condemned as not fit to be eaten by humans.

(i) Apart from being breathed in from the air, how else might radioactive material have entered the reindeer?

....

.... (1)

(ii) The main danger of radioactive material is that it can cause mutations. What is a mutation?

.... (1)

SEG 1991

4 (a) The table shows some information about what have become known as the 'greenhouse gases'.

Name	Source	Influence on greenhouse effect (%)
Carbon dioxide	burning forests burning fossil fuels cement production	56
CFCs (chlorofluorocarbons)	refrigerators air conditioning systems aerosol propellant	23
Methane	rotting vegetation waste gases from animals, e.g. cows, sheep	14
Nitrous oxide	breakdown of organic and inorganic fertilizers	7

3 Populations and human influences

QUESTIONS

(i) On the graph below plot the data showing the influence of each gas on the greenhouse effect. The percentage for carbon dioxide has already been plotted for you.

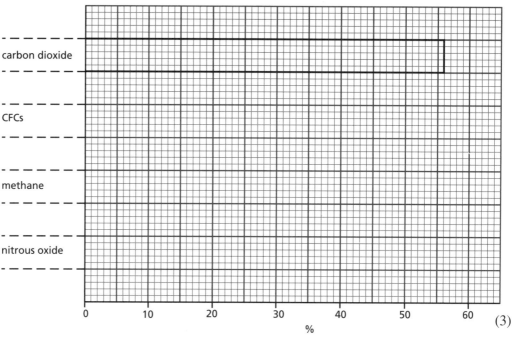

(3)

(ii) On the evidence in the table, which of the greenhouse gases are products of natural processes?

.... (2)

(iii) In light of the data in the table, suggest why the following should be encouraged:
1 the development of renewable energy devices such as windmills;
2 better insulation of houses;
3 planting more trees.

....

....

....

....

.... (6)

(b) In 1800 there were 280 parts per million of carbon dioxide in the atmosphere. In 1990 there were 350 parts per million and this is expected to rise to 560 by the year 2030.

(i) How much more carbon dioxide was in the air in 1990 compared to 1800?

.... (1)

Populations and human influences 3

(ii) The predicted rise in carbon dioxide concentration in the period from 1990 to 2030 is 310 parts per million.
Suggest an explanation for the difference between this value and your answer to (i).

....

....

.... (2)

MEG 1994

5 Last year, half a million tonnes of detergents were flushed into rivers in Britain. Most detergents contain phosphates which prevent the formation of scum on clothes. Some detergents contain enzymes. The use of phosphates in detergents is banned in Switzerland and Holland because cadmium is a by-product of phosphate production. This could reach water supplies. There are no controls in Britain despite this hazard of the heavy metal.

A substance called zeolite can be used instead of phosphate and has no side effects. When phosphates enter water, they can be used by algae and act as a fertilizer. Rivers and lakes can become 'over-fertile' and cause a dense blanket growth of algae on the surface of the river.

The composition of some detergents and information about their manufacture is shown in the following table:

Name	North Sea oil used in manufacture	Phosphate present	Enzymes present	Plant oils used in manufacture
Ariel	+	+	+	−
Bold	+	+	+	−
Ecover	−	−	−	+
Daz	+	+	+	−
Lux	−	−	−	−
Persil	−	+	+	−
Asda Auto	+	−	−	−
Tesco Auto	+	−	+	−

Key: +, yes; −, no.

(a) Name one detergent which would be banned in Holland.

.... (1)

(b) (i) Name one detergent which would be successful in boiling water.

.... (1)

(ii) Explain your answer to (i).

.... (1)

(c) Explain why the process of producing phosphate could be harmful to the environment.

....

37

3 Populations and human influences

QUESTIONS

....

.... (3)

(d) The production of which detergent uses a replaceable resource?

.... (1)

(e) Explain how a dense blanket of floating algae might affect the environment where the algae live.

....

....

.... (3)

(f) If you were a detergent manufacturer, explain how you would avoid environmental pollution and still prevent the formation of scum on clothes.

....

.... (1)

6 The production of sulphur dioxide in most of Europe has been reduced since 1980. This is shown on the map below, together with planned targets for reduction of sulphur dioxide by the year 2000.

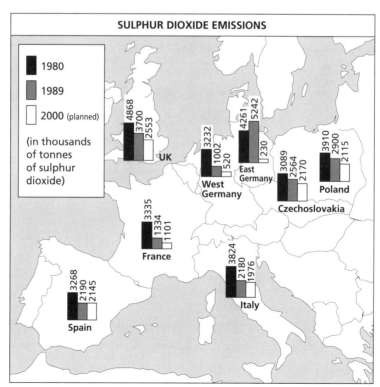

Populations and human influences 3

QUESTIONS

(a) (i) What percentage reduction in sulphur dioxide production was made by Britain between 1980 and 1989?

.... (1)

(ii) Which country was the biggest contributor to acid rain between 1980 and 1989?

.... (1)

(iii) Name the two countries which are closest to reaching their planned targets for the year 2000.

.... (1)

(b) Suggest a way of reducing sulphur dioxide emissions in the atmosphere while still maintaining the energy requirements of European countries.

.... (1)

(c) Explain concisely the effects of acid rain on (i) freshwater fish and (ii) trees.

....
....
....
....
....
.... (6)

4 Ecosystems

REVISION SUMMARY

All organisms depend on their surroundings to stay alive.

There is a thin layer of life starting a few feet below the ground and extending through the lower atmosphere of our planet. It is called the *biosphere*. It may be considered as one huge *ecosystem*. Or, it may be divided into many small ecosystems. An *ecosystem* is an environment in which living and non-living things affect one another. It is also a system in which materials are recycled. Living organisms are the community. Groups of the same kind of organisms are called populations.

The non-living part of the ecosystem is called the *physical environment* or *habitat*. It has much influence on the biotic community.

A stable population density is important to a balanced ecosystem. Many factors can change population density. Lack of food, for example, will cause a population to decrease. Removal of natural enemies will usually make it temporarily increase. These same factors influence human population density.

Physical factors of an environment (abiotic factors)

❶ Light intensity is particularly important because of its function in photosynthesis.

❷ Oxygen and carbon dioxide are important because of their functions in respiration and photosynthesis, respectively.

❸ Temperature is important because of the influence it has on the rate of chemical reactions going on in all living things.

❹ A balanced supply of minerals is essential to all living things as part of their nutrition.

❺ Water is essential because it makes up a large proportion of protoplasm and all chemical reactions in living things take place in solution.

Biotic factors

All living organisms have some influence upon the outside environment of their neighbours. This influence may be small, such as in a limited competition for water or light. On the other hand it may be very great. For example, many animals play an important part in the outside environment of plants. Some animals pollinate flowers; others disperse seeds; some are the carriers of plant disease; some trample vegetation. Among animals, humans have had the greatest impact on the environment of other organisms.

The total outside environment, consisting of both abiotic and biotic factors, determines which species come together to form a natural community in any one place.

Life in communities

Three sorts of relationships are recognized:

❶ **Competition**: may be between the many members of a given species, or between members of different species.

❷ **Dependence**: all animals are dependent on plants for a supply of food and oxygen.

❸ **Interdependence**: while some organisms compete with one another, and some are totally dependent upon others, there are some ways in which all the species in a community are interdependent.

If you need to revise this subject more thoroughly, see the relevant topics in the *Letts* GCSE *Biology* and *Human Biology Study Guides*.

Ecosystems 4

QUESTIONS

1 Study the food web below.

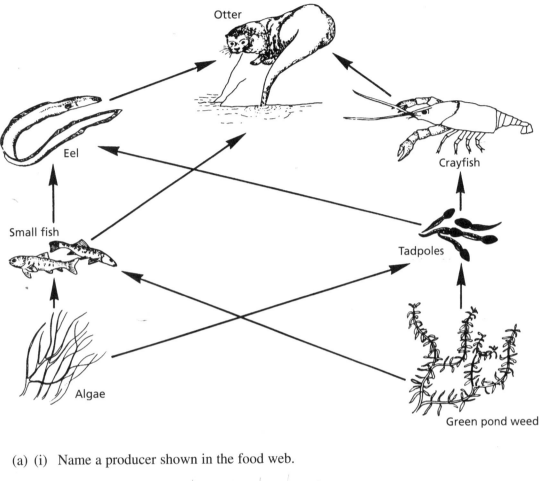

(a) (i) Name a producer shown in the food web.

.... (1)

(ii) What is the source of energy for the food web?

.... (1)

(iii) Not all of the energy converted by the producers reached the otter. Give **two** reasons for this energy loss.

Reason 1. ....

.... (1)

Reason 2. ....

.... (1)

4 Ecosystems

QUESTIONS

(b) An outbreak of Crayfish Plague killed all the crayfish in the river. State **three** effects the death of the crayfish would have on the other organisms in the food web shown.

....

....

.... (3)

(c) Pesticides containing toxic substances entered the water from local farm land. Explain why some otters died but the other animals were less affected.

....

....

....

.... (4)

NEAB 1994

2 On a group of islands, numbers of sea birds called kittiwakes, puffins, terns and skuas have been greatly reduced. In 1981 there were 54 000 kittiwakes, but now only a few hundred remain. The sea birds' main food is sand eels, which are caught in large numbers for use as food in dairy and fish farms on the islands.
The sand eel population has decreased rapidly.

(a) (i) Suggest one reason why the number of birds has decreased.

.... (1)

(ii) What could be done immediately to stop the decrease in the numbers of birds?

.... (1)

(iii) What effect would this step have on the people of the islands?

.... (1)

(b) The farmers claim that there is no evidence to prove that the sand eel fishing is to blame for the decrease in bird population. As a scientist, how would you set up a long-term experiment to obtain evidence?

....

....

....

.... (4)

42

Ecosystems 4

QUESTIONS

3 In France, early attempts at making nitrates for use in the production of gun powder consisted of trickling nitrate-free water through heaps of decaying carcasses of animals, excretory products and soil. After a few days, the water passing out of these heaps contained nitrate. It was noticed that when chlorine was added to the heaps of decaying material no nitrate was formed.

(a) What was the purpose of adding soil?

.... (1)

(b) Explain how nitrate was formed.

....

....

....

.... (4)

(c) State why chlorine prevented nitrates forming.

.... (1)

(d) Once nitrogen is made available to plants in the form of nitrates, explain what happens to it.

....

.... (2)

4 The flow chart represents energy flow through an ecosystem.

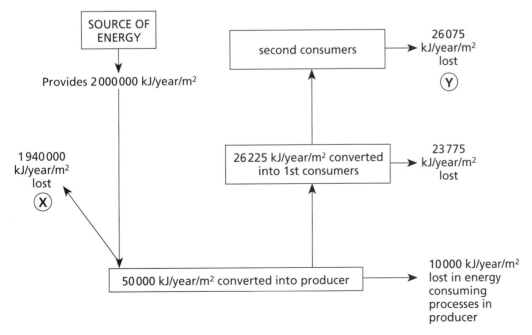

4 Ecosystems

QUESTIONS

(a) Calculate the energy gained by the second consumers per unit area per year.

　.. (1)

(b) Suggest two ways in which energy is lost at point X.

　(i) ....

　(ii) .... (2)

(c) Suggest two ways in which energy is lost at point Y.

　(i) ....

　(ii) .... (2)

(d) Calculate the percentage of the energy lost at point X.

　.. (1)

(e) Explain why a one hectare field of maize would yield more energy for human use than cattle in a field of the same area.

　..

　.. (2)

44

Human Biology 5

Human reproduction

Functions of the male reproductive organs

Structure	Function
Testes	Production of sperm
Scrotal sacs	Contain the testes; they maintain the temperature of the testes slightly below normal body temperature, which is necessary for development and survival of sperm
Vas deferens	Tubes which conduct the sperm to the urethra by peristalsis
Penis	For insertion into the vagina to release sperm at the cervix of the uterus
Prostate gland and seminal vesicles	Secretion of seminal fluid, which acts as a lubricant and nutritive medium for the sperm
Urethra	A tube running through the penis which carries both sperm (during copulation) and urine (during urination)

Functions of the female reproductive organs

Structure	Function
Ovaries	Production of eggs (ova)
Uterus (or womb)	Plays a part in development of the embryo and formation of the placenta
Cervix	The opening to the uterus for the passage of sperm during copulation. The baby emerges through the cervix during birth
Vagina	For the reception of the penis during copulation For the passage of the baby during birth
Fallopian tubes (oviducts)	Provide the ideal environment for fertilization to take place Conduct the fertilized egg to the uterus
Urethra	For the passage of urine from the bladder

REVISION SUMMARY

Sperms are many, minute and mobile. The **ovum** is very large compared to the sperm. It contains the food for the early life stages of the *zygote*. Several *hormones* produced by the female co-ordinate the development of the ovum and the wall of the *uterus*. If fertilization does not occur, the soft uterine vascular lining is shed during *menstruation*. The entire cycle takes about 28 days.

If fertilization does occur, the zygote travels down the *fallopian tube* to the *uterus*. It becomes a many-celled sphere surrounded by the first of four membranes. The *embryo* then becomes attached to the uterine lining by the *placenta*. The diagram on the next page shows the stages involved, which are as follows:

❶ Ovary produces egg

❷ Egg released into fallopian tube

❸ At about the same time, sperm enter vagina

❹ Sperm swim up through uterus

❺ Sperm swim along fallopian tube

❻ Sperm make contact with the egg

❼ Single sperm and egg fuse – fertilization

❽ Fertilized egg, now divided into 4 cells, is conducted towards uterus

5 Human Biology

REVISION SUMMARY

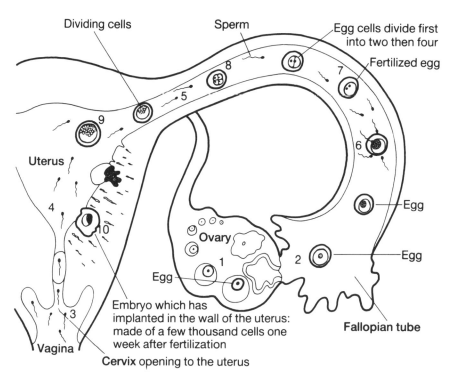

The fate of an egg

❾ Fertilized egg about to implant in wall of uterus

❿ Implantation complete, the placenta starts to develop

Summary of the hormonal control of the female reproductive cycle:

❶ Pituitary gland secretes follicle-stimulating hormone (FSH) which causes the eggs to grow inside Graafian follicles within the ovaries.

❷ Graafian follicles secrete the hormone oestrogen.

❸ Oestrogen causes the lining of the uterus to become thick and glandular. It also stops FSH production and causes the production of another pituitary hormone, luteinizing hormone (LH).

❹ LH causes an egg to be shed from an ovary and causes the corresponding Graafian follicle to grow from the corpus luteum (yellow body).

❺ The corpus luteum is an endocrine gland, secreting a hormone, progesterone. Progesterone prepares the uterus for reception and development of the embryo and stops the secretion of LH.

The foetus is totally dependent on the placenta for oxygen and nourishment. These materials are transferred by diffusion through the thin membranes. The blood of the mother and foetus do not mix. At the time the baby is born, changes in its circulatory and breathing systems allow it to breathe and become physically independent.

If you need to revise this subject more thoroughly, see the relevant topics in the Letts GCSE Biology and Human Biology Study Guides.

Growth

Growth is an irreversible increase in size of an organism involving the *synthesis of protoplasm*. It begins at the moment of *fertilization*, continues through *gestation* (the period spent in the womb), and goes on until the end of *adolescence*. In many cases there is no further growth, although all parts of the body change and develop. Some parts of the body, such as the brain, *regress* until the end of life. The importance of growth before birth is illustrated by the fact that the fertilized egg divides 44 times between conception and its appearance as a baby. From then until adulthood only four more divisions occur.

46

Human Biology 5

QUESTIONS

1 The graph represents the rate of height increase for boys from one to seventeen years of age.

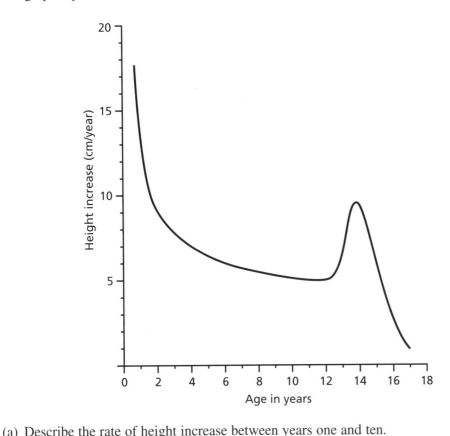

(a) Describe the rate of height increase between years one and ten.

   ....

   .... (2)

(b) What name is commonly given to the period represented by the small peak between thirteen and fifteen years?

   .... (1)

(c) State **three** other changes that are taking place in the male body during this period.

   ....

   ....

   .... (3)

(d) State **two** changes you would expect to be taking place in the female body from the age of ten to thirteen years.

   ....

   .... (2)

5 Human Biology

QUESTIONS

2 The graph shows how the uterus lining varies in thickness with time. Fertilization took place on the 16th day of the second menstrual cycle.

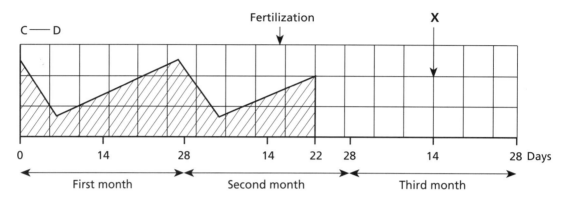

(a) State the process which took place between C and D.

   .... (1)

(b) Complete the graph to point X to show what happens to the lining of the uterus after day 22 in the second month. (1)

(c) Explain why it is important that the uterus lining changes in the way shown.

   ....

   .... (2)

(d) Describe what happens to the zygote from the time it is formed until implantation occurs.

   .... (2)

(e) If the oviducts (Fallopian tubes) are blocked, a woman cannot have a baby in the normal way, but may be able to have a 'test tube' baby. In order for this to happen, a doctor pushes a fine tube through the body wall and takes several eggs from the ovary.

   Why can't the eggs be obtained through the vagina and uterus?

   .... (1)

(f) The eggs are then put into a small glass dish and sperm are mixed with them. After a few days the developing zygotes are put back into the woman's uterus through the cervix.

   (i) Why are sperm mixed with the eggs before they are put back into the woman?

   ....

   .... (2)

48

Human Biology 5

(ii) Explain why the zygotes are kept for a few days before they are put back into the woman.

.... (1)

(g) Give two reasons why the term 'test tube baby' is misleading.

(i) ....

(ii) .... (2)

(h) Name three changes which take place in the uterus to help protect and nourish the developing embryo.

....

....

.... (3)

3 The diagram below shows an embryo and its blood supply.

(a) Explain two ways in which the structure of the placenta enables it to carry out its functions.

(i) ....

.... (1)

49

5 Human Biology

QUESTIONS

(ii) ....

.... (1)

(b) It is important for the chemical composition of the blood of the embryo to remain constant. Explain how carbon dioxide, oxygen and urea enter the blood of the embryo, how they are transported, and how they are removed from the blood.

(i) Carbon dioxide

....

....

.... (3)

(ii) Oxygen

....

....

.... (3)

(iii) Urea

....

....

.... (3)

4 The following diagram shows red bone marrow tissue producing mutant cells after exposure to radioactivity. The mutant cells multiply in an uncontrolled way and become cancerous.

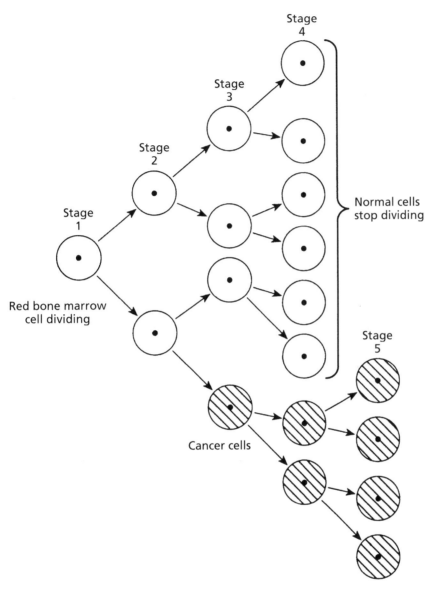

(a) If the cell in stage 1 had 46 chromosomes, how many chromosomes are in a cell from stage 2?

.... (1)

(b) (i) Between which two stages has mutation taken place?

Between stage .... and stage .... (1)

(ii) What is meant by the term 'mutation'?

....

.... (1)

5 Human Biology

QUESTIONS

(c) Explain how genetic mutation can arise from the effects of radioactivity.

....

....

.... (2)

5 (a) (i) The diagram shows a single strand of DNA. Using the same symbols as in the diagram, add the missing bases.

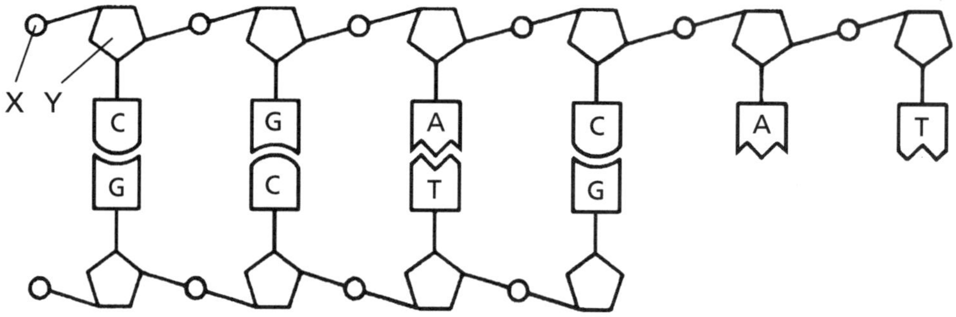

(1)

(ii) What do X and Y in the diagram represent?

X ....

Y .... (1)

(iii) How are the bases held together?

.... (1)

(b) Analysis of a sample of DNA showed 33% of the bases were guanine (G on the diagram). Calculate the percentage of the bases in the sample which would be adenine (A on the diagram). Explain how you arrived at your answer.

....

....

.... (3)

(c) Explain the meaning and the function of the genetic code.

....

....

.... (3)

Plant Biology 6

REVISION SUMMARY

Flowering plant reproduction

Plants can *reproduce* themselves in two ways. When they *propagate vegetatively*, they send out long stems, either above or below the ground. These stems eventually put down their own *roots*, develop independent *shoots*, and become separate plants. *Grafting* and *budding* are artificial means of vegetative propagation.

Sexual reproduction is the other way plants propagate their species. It provides a vital means of adapting to a changing environment through variations from one generation to the next. The *flower* of the plant contains the parts needed for sexual reproduction.

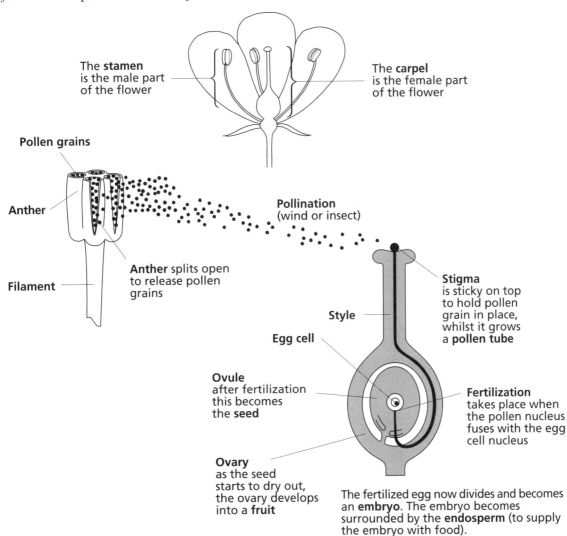

Water balance in plants

To survive, an organism must remain in a state of balance with its environment. An important factor for this balance is the movement of materials in and out of cells. All of this traffic must pass through the *cell membrane*.

The cell membrane is *selectively permeable* i.e. different molecules and ions pass through it at different rates. Foods, water, wastes, and other materials can pass through the membrane. The materials of the cell structures themselves are kept within the cell membrane.

The forces of *diffusion* control the movement of molecules and other particles through the membrane. Diffusion of water is called **osmosis**. No cell energy is used in diffusion. For this reason, movement of molecules by diffusion is called *passive transport*. In some cases, cells absorb ions against the force of diffusion. Cell energy is used in this process, which is known as *active transport*. Large molecules cannot pass through membrane pores. Instead, they flow into pouches in the membrane and are sealed off. They then enter the cell as *vacuoles*.

If you need to revise this subject more thoroughly, see the relevant topics in the *Letts* GCSE Biology Study Guide.

6 Plant Biology

QUESTIONS

1. A pupil carried out a series of experiments on seeds. The diagrams show a piece of apparatus she used for an investigation.

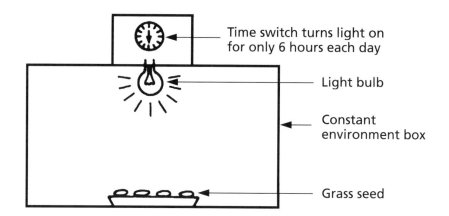

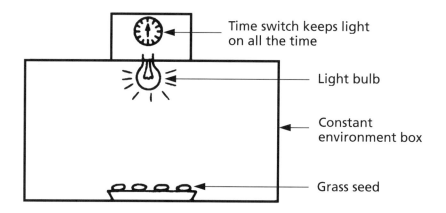

(a) What could have been the aim of this investigation?

.... (1)

(b) State three factors necessary for germination which the constant environment box must supply.

....

....

.... (3)

(c) Suggest how she should set up another environment box for a valid conclusion.

.... (1)

Plant Biology

QUESTIONS

2 A plant was treated as shown in the diagram.

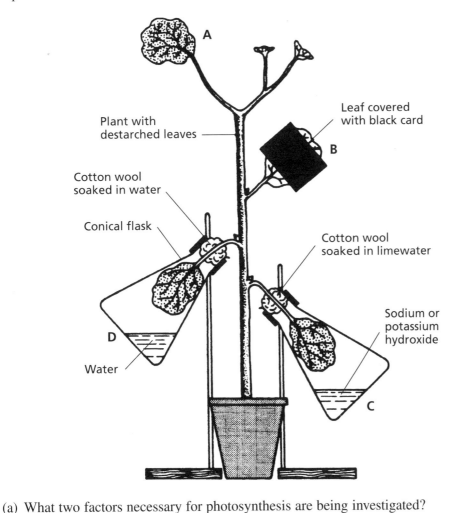

(a) What two factors necessary for photosynthesis are being investigated?

....

.... (2)

(b) (i) Which two of the leaves shown would you use as controls.

....

.... (2)

(ii) Give reasons for your choice.

Leaf ....

Reason .... (1)

Leaf ....

Reason .... (1)

6 Plant Biology

QUESTIONS

(c) Explain concisely what happens to the starch in the plant during the process of destarching.

....

....

.... (3)

3 (a) The diagram below shows parts of a flower.

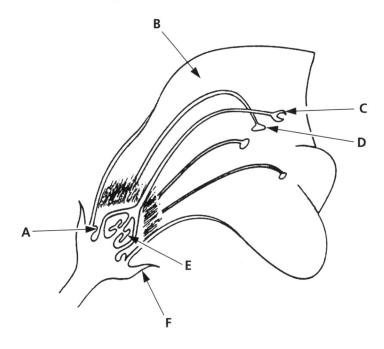

(i) Use the letters from the diagram to match the **structures** in Table 1 and to match the **functions** in Table 2.

Table 1

Structure	Letter
Nectary	
Ovary	
Stigma	

(2)

Table 2

Function	Letter
Produces pollen	
Protects the flower when in bud	

(1)

(ii) Name the method of pollination used by this flower.

Method of pollination .... (1)

(b) Three twigs from the same plant, with leaves of equal surface area, were set up as shown in the diagram below.

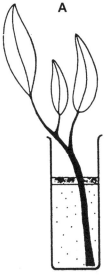
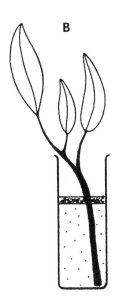
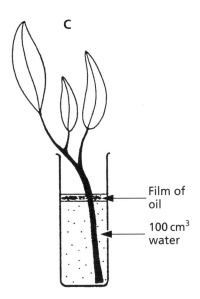

Upper leaf surfaces covered in vaseline

Lower leaf surfaces covered in vaseline

Neither leaf surfaces covered in vaseline

The experiments were left in identical environmental conditions for 48 hours.

The results in the table below show the volume of water remaining in each cylinder.

Cylinder	Volume of water remaining (cm³)
A	76
B	90
C	65

(i) Calculate the rate of water loss per hour from the leaves in cylinder A.

Rate of water loss .... cm³/hour (1)

(ii) The leaf surfaces contain pores through which water vapour is lost. Name these pores. Give **one** other function of these pores.

Name .... (1)

Function ....

.... (1)

6 Plant Biology

(iii) Covering the leaf surface with vaseline blocks the leaf pores.

What conclusion can you come to about the number of pores in the upper and lower leaf surfaces of this plant?

....

.... (1)

(iv) Apart from being from the same plant, state **one** other feature of the leaves which **must** be the same so that the comparison of the results is fair.

....

.... (1)

(v) If oil was not added to the cylinders, the results obtained would be inaccurate. Why would this be the case.

....

.... (1)

SEB 1994

4   Two students investigated how the mass of slices of potato changed when in different concentrations of sugar solution. The slices were weighed, placed in different concentrations of sugar for 30 minutes, then weighed again without drying.
The results are shown in the table below.

Concentration of sugar solution (g per dm³)	Mass of slice at start (g)	Mass of slice after 30 mins. (g)	% change in mass of slice
1	3.60	4.02	+11.7
40	3.20	3.32	+3.9
60	3.10	3.10	0
80	3.05	2.96	−2.8
120	3.64	3.33	−8.5

+, a mass increase −, a mass decrease.

(a) Explain the changes in the masses of the potato slices in the following sugar solutions:

(i) 1 g per dm³

....

....

.... (2)

Plant Biology 6

QUESTIONS

    (ii) 120 g per dm³

    ....

    ....

    .... (2)

(b) (i) Which sugar concentration was most similar to the concentration of the cell sap of the potato?

    .... (1)

    (ii) Explain your answer.

    ....

    .... (1)

(c) (i) Suggest an error which the students should have avoided to obtain valid results.

    .... (1)

    (ii) State why you think it was an error.

    .... (1)

    (iii) Describe how the error could have been prevented.

    ....

    .... (1)

(d) In the experiment the students calculated the percentage mass gain or loss. Why was this better than simply using the actual mass gain or loss?

    .... (1)

(e) Explain why there was no change in mass of boiled potato slices when these were used for the same investigation as described.

    ....

    .... (1)

Answers

1 LIFE PROCESSES

Question	Answer	Mark

1 (a) (i) A liver   C stomach
   B large intestine   D small intestine   **4** (One mark each)

> **Examiner's tip** Use only the words from the list.

(ii) X just below the stomach   **1**

> **Examiner's tip** Do not make the X too large, as this might suggest that you are not sure about the exact position.

(iii) enzymes
alkaline solution
insulin   **2** (Any 2)

(b) gastric juice — fluid containing enzymes and hydrochloric acid
peristalsis — a wave of muscular contraction
bile — fluid made in the liver, stored in the gall bladder   **3** (One mark each)

> **Examiner's tip** Notice the one extra description in the question. This is to avoid you reaching the correct answer by luck.

(c) No villi on inner surface   **1**
therefore less surface area   **1**
so less glucose absorbed into the blood.   **1**
Cow slowly dies through starvation.   **1**

> **Examiner's tip** You are not expected to know about the 'cow disease'. However, you should be able to relate the information you understand about digestion into this context.

(d) It makes the food in our gut soft and moist   **1**
so it can move along quickly and easily.   **1**
Without fibre we would become constipated.   **1**
This can eventually damage the gut.   **1**
Lack of fibre can cause piles, appendicitis and cancer.   **1**
(Any 3)

> **Examiner's tip** This is the last part of the question and you are expected to write a more detailed answer, showing what you know and understand.

Answers to Unit 1

Question	Answer	Mark
2 (a) (i)	All 11 co-ordinates plotted correctly.	3
	Between 10 and 8 co-ordinates plotted correctly.	2
	Between 7 and 5 co-ordinates plotted correctly.	1
	Less than 5 co-ordinates plotted correctly.	0

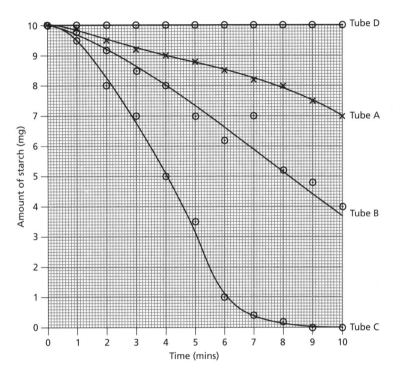

Examiner's tip Take care. Plotting co-ordinates is expected to be carried out accurately. Use either a ⊕ or a ✳

(ii)	Smooth curve joining most co-ordinates.	2
	OR Dot-to-dot line joining all/most co-ordinates.	1

Examiner's tip The line is to show the pattern or trend of the results. You are not expected to join all of the dots, only those that occur within the general pattern. The co-ordinate at 7 minutes was an obvious mistake and should not be included.

(b) (i)	40 °C	1
(ii)	9 minutes	1

Examiner's tip This answer can be obtained either from the graph or the results tables. Take care to read the correct set of readings: tube C.

(iii)	Maltose	1
	Amylase	1

Examiner's tip You did not need to know about this particular enzyme reaction to answer this part of the question. With your understanding of enzymes you know that the enzyme would not be broken down, it just changes the rate of reaction. The start of the question provides the other part of the answer as maltose.

Answers to Unit 1

Question	Answer	Mark
(c)	The high temperature denatures the enzyme.	2

Examiner's tip An answer such as 'Stops it working' is a vague statement and so is only worth 1 mark.

(d)	The enzymes in biological washing powders will work most effectively at an optimum temperature.	1
	The optimum temperature for protein-digesting enzymes will be approximately 37 °C.	1
	As shown by the graph.	1
	Therefore temperature of wash should be no higher than 40 °C.	1
	If the temperature is too high the enzyme will be denatured and become less effective.	1
		(Any 3)

Examiner's tip The answer 'Wash at a low temperature' is too vague and would only be credited with 1 mark.

3	(a)	(i) Photosynthesis or storage of chlorophyll.	1
		(ii) X Oxygen	1
		Y Carbon dioxide	1
	(b)	Lack of light causes a leaf to develop a larger surface area	1
		to capture the maximum amount of light available for photosynthesis.	1

Examiner's tip 'Larger surface area' is a useful term. The word 'bigger' would not gain marks.

	(c)	A large surface area for diffusion.	1
		Moist surface area because gases have to diffuse in solution.	1
		A thin surface area so that gases can diffuse through them.	1
			(Any two)
	(d)	Lungs have a blood supply to take oxygen away from the surface and to take carbon dioxide to the surface. Leaves do not.	1
		Lungs have tubes (bronchioles) to take the air to the surface but leaves do not.	1

Examiner's tip An answer stating 'lungs have blood' or 'lungs have tubes' would not gain marks. You need to develop your answer to state why the blood and tubes are there. Do not forget this is the end of the question and so you need to give more detail to earn your marks.

4	(a)	(i) A Humerus	
		B Ligament	
		C Synovial fluid	
		D Ulna	2
			(All four correct 2 marks
			Three correct 1 mark)

62

Answers to Unit 1

Question	Answer	Mark
(ii)	Part B holds bones in place at a joint.	1

Examiner's tip Even if you did not know the name of B you could still answer this question.

(iii)	See diagram	2

Diagram showing radius and cartilage at a joint.

(iv)	It has smooth slippery cartilage	1
	and lubricating synovial fluid.	1

Examiner's tip Notice the description, 'slippery', 'lubricating', as well as stating the name of the part.

(v)	The biceps muscle contracts to raise the lower arm	1
	while the triceps relaxes.	1
	They can be said to work antagonistically to one another.	1
		(Any 2 points)
(b)	The metal joint does not have any ligaments	1
	or synovial fluid	1
	or cartilage.	1

Examiner's tip Do not become involved with a vague answer such as the shape of the bones, i.e. the humerus is rounded, but is not so in the artificial joint. Provide more obvious answers such as the three given.

5 (a)	Regulation of the body's internal environment.	1

Examiner's tip Definitions need to be learned. A lot of the questions can be answered by understanding, but you must learn definitions.

(b)	Glucose, amino acids, vitamins, urea, iron.	1
		(Any one of these would gain 1 mark)
(c)	Insulin	1
	Glucagon	1
(d)	Insulin removes glucose from the blood	1
	by helping to change it to glycogen	
	or by speeding up its use in respiration.	1

Answers to Unit 1

Question	Answer	Mark
	Glucagon balances the action of insulin by putting glucose back into the blood when it is needed	1
	by helping to change glycogen into glucose.	1
(e)	If glucose concentration drops below a certain critical level, the body would not have sufficient energy for all of the actions that it has to perform.	1

Examiner's tip Do not give specific examples here as the answer is only worth one mark.

(f)

A Increase in concentration of glucose 1

B .... Insulin .... 1 release from the pancreas

C .... glucose .... 1 Decrease in concentration of

D Decrease in production of insulin 1

6 (a) (i) X in correct place. 1

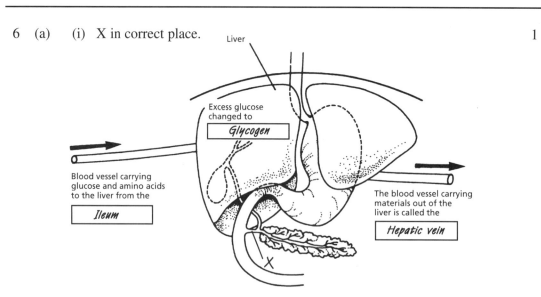

(ii) Correct label in each box. 3
(1 mark for each)

(b)

Class of food	Chemical elements present	
Carbohydrate	Carbon, hydrogen, oxygen	
Protein	Carbon, hydrogen, oxygen, nitrogen	1
Fat	Carbon, hydrogen, oxygen	1

Answers to Unit 1

Question	Answer	Mark

> **Examiner's tip** Often the first part of a table is completed for you. This should give you guidance to the type of answer expected.

(c) Can help break down large molecules (iii) — 1

> **Examiner's tip** The other answers can be correctly applied to enzymes but the question states 'are essential'. Therefore only (iii) is the correct answer.

(d) D — 1

7 (a) In the USA, the more blood cholesterol present in humans, the more likely they are to die of coronary heart disease. — 1

(b) At the age of about 55 women stop producing oestrogen. — 1
This normally prevents cholesterol being deposited inside arteries. — 1
Up to the age of 55 there is less chance of women suffering from coronary heart disease. — 1
Over this age LDLs exert their effect and there are no HDLs there to counteract it. — 1
This increases their chances of suffering from coronary heart disease. — 1
(Any four)

> **Examiner's tip** You will not have been taught about LDLs or HDLs. You are expected to use the information at the start of the question and shown in the graph.

(c) Stress, smoking, drinking excess alcohol. — 2 (Any two)

8 (a) (i) Y — 1
(ii) W — 1
(iii) Z — 1

(b)

Substance or cell	Dialysis fluid
Salts	+
Urea	
Glucose	+
Proteins	
Water	+
Blood cells	

1

1

> **Examiner's tip** Note that salts and glucose must be added so that the concentration of these substances on either side of the dialysis membrane is the same. This would prevent an unequal net flow of these materials in any one direction.

(c) Fluid A: dialysis fluid — 1
Fluid B: W — 1

65

Answers to Unit 1

Question	Answer	Mark
(d) (i)	Less long-term cost *or* less inconvenience *or* lack of mobility when frequently using a kidney machine.	1
(ii)	Difficulties with rejection *or* tissue matching *or* obtaining suitable donors.	1

2 INHERITANCE AND EVOLUTION

Question	Answer	Mark
1 (a)	KEY H = hairy h = hairless	1
	Parental genotypes Hh × Hh	1

First Cross

	H	h
H	HH	Hh
h	hH	hh

1

Examiner's tip The question said original parents, which were normal hairy (but produced a hairless variety), so the cross must be Hh × Hh.

Second Cross

	H	h
h	hH	hh
h	hH	hh

1

Examiner's tip Now use hh to increase the numbers of hairless.

(b) (i)	HH × HH	1
(ii)	HH × Hh	1
(iii)	HH × hh	1
(c)	Male = XY Female = XX	1

Examiner's tip You need to get both parts correct for one mark.

	X	Y
X	XX	XY
X	XX	XY

1

66

Answers to Unit 2

Question			Answer	Mark
2	(a)		There will be a different number of chromosomes.	1
			The removed nucleus contains half the number of chromosomes or only single chromosomes.	1
			This can be expressed by saying that the haploid (not the diploid) number of chromosomes will be in the nucleus that is removed.	1
	(b)		The unfertilized eggs of frogs or toads are bigger	1
			so they are easier to manipulate and remove the nucleus.	1

Examiner's tip You could also gain the marks by stating that the eggs of frogs or toads are passed out of the adults and are therefore easier to obtain.

	(c)	(i)	Rabbit B	1
		(ii)	It will have identical genes or chromosomes	1
			and will therefore have identical genetical information to rabbit B.	1
	(d)		(Stage 2) nucleus removed	1
			(Stage 3) liver or body cell from breed B	1
			(Stage 4) nucleus transferred	1
			(Stage 5) egg placed in womb of breed A	1

Examiner's tip If you read the introduction to the question most of this information was supplied. So even if you did not know about cloning in animals, you could still gain some marks.

	(e)		Advantages: All the clones would be identical and will have the same desirable features.	1
			A good rate of weight gain or fleece quality would be a good example.	1
			Disadvantages: All the clones would be identical and will have the same poor features.	1
			Susceptibility to the same illnesses or diseases would be a good example.	1
			OR	
			This procedure would result in less variety of animals	1
			and valuable genes for desirable characteristics may be lost.	1
	(f)	(i)	Evolution or natural selection or genetic mutation	1
		(ii)	Any six of the following:	
			Some individuals had genes for longer necks.	
			Long-necked individuals were at an advantage.	
			They could reach food growing at a greater height on trees.	
			They could see predators with their higher eyes.	
			They were more likely to survive to breed.	
			Their offspring would inherit the advantageous genes from the parents.	
			Others would die out.	
			These selective pressures of the environment would lead to evolution	
			by natural selection of the fittest to breed.	6 × 1

Examiner's tip This part of the question carries 6 marks, so careful planning is needed. Write out your ideas in rough first. Select 6 main points and write them out neatly for your answer. Do not forget to cross out your notes.

67

Answers to Unit 2

Question	Answer	Mark
3 (a)	C D B E A	1
(b)	Bacteria divide quickly to form large colonies. As bacteria reproduce asexually they pass on an identical copy of the new gene to the cells in the colony.	1

Examiner's tip As this is taken from a Credit level paper, both of your answers to (b) need to be correct and complete to earn the mark. Half marks are not usually awarded.

4 (a)	Reproductive/gamete/sex cell.	1
(b)	If a gene controls a helpful character	1
	it is selected as an adaptation or responds to selective pressures of the environment.	1
	The gene is passed on to future generations during sexual reproduction.	1
5 (a)	Numbers correctly inserted on diagram.	2

46 (Adult female) → 46 (Female sex organs) —A→ 23 (Female gamete) —B→ 46 (Zygote) —C→ 46 (Foetus); X labels Female sex organs; 23 Male gamete joins at B; Z labels after zygote.

Examiner's tip The gametes always have half the usual number of chromosomes, so when they come together the correct number of chromosomes is present.

(b) (i)	Meiosis	1
(ii)	Mitosis	1
(iii)	Fertilization	1
(c) (i)&(ii)	See diagram	2

Examiner's tip Use a labelling line to help you mark the point. Do not use more than one labelling line just because you are not sure. This would result in no marks.

3 POPULATIONS AND HUMAN INFLUENCES

Question	Answer	Mark
1 (a)	0.9 million per year	1

Examiner's tip 4.5 million in 0–5 age group for country A divided by 5 as range covers five years.

68

Answers to Unit 3

Question	Answer	Mark
(b)	66–70 years	1

Examiner's tip Initial population is 4.5 million. 50% of 4.5 million is 2.25 million. The age range 66–70 years is closest to a population of 2.25 million, i.e. when 50% of initial population is still alive.

(c) Number of women aged 15–45 = 11.7 million   1

$$\frac{0.9 \text{ million}}{11.7 \text{ million}} \times 1000$$ 1

= 76.9   1

Examiner's tip If you were incorrect on your calculation of 0.9 million, but everything else is correct, you can still score 2 marks.

(d) Any six of the following: Mass vaccination. Mass X-raying. Insect vector control. Agricultural pest control. Improved fertilizers. Disease resistant crops. High yield crops. Improved irrigation. Provision of contraception.   6 × 1

Examiner's tip As this answer is worth 6 marks, you would need to plan your answer. You can ask for extra paper in an examination or you can write your notes in a space on the examination paper, but be sure to cross them out afterwards. Check you have listed 6 points, one for each mark.

2 (a) (i) Stratosphere   1
     (ii) CFCs   1

Examiner's tip This information is shown in the diagram.

(b) (i) CFCs   1
     chlorine   1
     oxygen   1

(ii) Too much ultraviolet radiation (harmful sunrays) from the sun will reach the Earth.   1
Increase in the risk of skin cancer;
or eye cataracts (eye damage);
or possible breakdown of immune system.   1

(c) Any two of:
Reduction in the use of spray cans containing CFCs.
Reduction in the use of CFCs in fridges and freezers
(*or* more careful disposal of old fridges/freezers).
Reduction in the use of CFCs to make plastic foams.
Research into alternatives to CFCs.
Research into reforming ozone.   2

Examiner's tip A vague answer such as 'fewer aerosols' or 'ozone friendly aerosols' would not gain credit unless the reduction of CFCs was explained.

Answers to Unit 3

Question	Answer	Mark
3 (a) (i)	The direction of the wind on that day.	1

Examiner's tip Do not be too vague, an answer of 'wind' might not be sufficient to earn credit.

(ii) Any one of:
Rain, precipitation, snow, hail, radioactive material is heavy and would return to earth. **1**

(b) (i) The radioactive material settled on the lichens, which were then eaten by the reindeer. **1**

Examiner's tip You could go on to explain that radioactive material is accumulative and, once inside the reindeer, would not pass out of their bodies.

(ii) A sudden change in an individual gene. **1**

4 (a) (i) 1 mark for each correctly drawn bar on the graph. **3**

(ii) methane **1**
nitrous oxide **1**

Examiner's tip The question did not ask for two gases; however, the question did refer to 'gases' and the (2) indicates two marks available. If you were unsure and wrote more than two gases for your answer you would lose marks. For every extra incorrect answer given one mark is cancelled from your total for that part of the question.

(iii) If there were more renewable energy devices such as windmills in operation then less fossil fuel would need to be burned in the electricity generating process. If homes were better insulated then less fuel would be needed to heat the houses.
Both of these examples would reduce the amount of carbon dioxide entering the atmosphere. Carbon dioxide has the largest influence on the greenhouse effect.
If homes were better insulated there would also be less use of air conditioning systems. These systems contain CFCs, which also have an influence on the greenhouse effect.
Green plants take in carbon dioxide as they photosynthesize; therefore, if more trees were planted, more carbon dioxide would be removed from the atmosphere. Carbon dioxide has a major influence on the greenhouse effect. **6**

Examiner's tip When you study this question you will notice that there are three statements to discuss and six marks available. The answer to each statement, if extended, is worth two marks. If the answer is correct, but vague or too brief, then only one mark would be awarded.
This type of answer would only be credited with three marks:
Renewable energy should be used so less electricity is made. Houses need to be better insulated so less fuel is used for central heating. If more trees were planted more carbon dioxide would be removed from the atmosphere.

Answers to Unit 3

Question			Answer	Mark
	(b)	(i)	350 280 − ――― 70 parts per million	1
		(ii)	In the year 2030 the population will be much greater, therefore: there will be a greater demand for electricity and more fossil fuels will be burned. *or* more buildings will be needed so there will be an increase in the amount of cement being produced and more forests will be destroyed to create space for housing and crops. These factors will increase the amount of carbon dioxide in the atmosphere.	1 1
5	(a)		Ariel/Bold/Daz/Persil	1 (any one)
	(b)	(i)	Ecover/Lux/Asda Auto	1 (any one)
		(ii)	These do not contain enzymes. Enzymes are denatured by boiling.	1
	(c)		The production of phosphate uses cadmium. Cadmium is a heavy metal. It could build up in food chains to a toxic level.	1 1 1
	(d)		Ecover. The manufacture of this uses plant oils which are replaceable.	1
	(e)		In a dense blanket of algae, those plants at the bottom of the blanket would not receive light and would die. Bacteria will cause these to decay. The bacteria will use oxygen in the water and cause all aerobic life to suffer.	1 1 1
	(f)		Use zeolite as a substitute to phosphate. This would not harm the environment.	1

Examiner's tip Note that this question tests comprehension and application of knowledge of pollution of water by phosphates and the heavy metal cadmium.

6	(a)	(i)	24%	1

Examiner's tip 4868 − 3700 = 1168. (1168 ÷ 4868) × 100 = 24%

		(ii)	East Germany	1
		(iii)	Spain and Italy	1

Examiner's tip Both are needed for the mark

	(b)		The use of electrostatic precipitators *or* desulphurization flue extractors *or* the use of an alternative form of generating electricity besides fossil fuels, e.g. nuclear power or wind energy.	1

Answers to Unit 3

Question	Answer	Mark

Examiner's tip Note that any suggestions for an alternative source of energy must be realistic. For example, solar energy would only be appropriate in a suitable climate.

(c) (i) The acid in lakes releases aluminium ions and heavy metal ions from salts dissolved in water. — 1
These affect the membranes of fish eggs and prevent them hatching. — 1
They also affect the gills of the fish and prevent them breathing. — 1

(ii) The acidity of the soil — 1
releases aluminium ions — 1
which poison the roots of the trees. — 1

4 ECOSYSTEMS

Question	Answer	Mark

1 (a) (i) Green pond weed *or* algae. — 1

(ii) The Sun. — 1

(iii) Any two from:
Some energy is lost as each organism moves.
Some energy is lost through respiration.
Energy is lost through excretion.
Not all of the organism is eaten, i.e. bones left undigested. — 2

Examiner's tip Vague answers like 'the energy was used up' would not earn credit.

(b) Any three from:
More tadpoles.
Fewer green plants and algae because of more tadpoles.
Eels will face no competition for the tadpoles.
Otters will eat more eels and small fish or move out of the area in search of more food. — 3

(c) The small amounts of toxic substances did not affect other animals lower down the food chain. — 1
However the build up of substances in the otter caused death. — 1
Concentration of toxic substances increases as they pass through the food chain. — 2

2 (a) (i) A reason could be that there was less food for them due to over-fishing. — 1
Another could be that they were affected by a disease — 1
or by pollution. — 1
(Any 1)

(ii) A decrease in fishing sand eels would stop the decrease in the numbers of birds. — 1

(iii) This would affect the dairy industry and the fish farming industry on the island and could lead to unemployment. — 1

72

Answers to Unit 4

Question	Answer	Mark
(b)	In order to investigate the claim that sand eel fishing is to blame for the decrease in birds, the scientist should carry out the following steps:	
	Make accurate counts of the population of birds.	1
	Ban fishing sand eels for 2 years.	1
	Make accurate counts of the sea birds after the ban.	1
	An increase or a decrease in the population could then be determined.	1

Examiner's tip You would need to plan this answer out in rough first and check that you have 4 main points. Then write your answer out neatly.

Examiner's tip You are expected to apply your knowledge of the nitrogen cycle in this question. You are not expected to know about 'gun powder production'.

3 (a)	To provide bacteria for the nitrogen cycle	1
(b)	Putrefying bacteria	1
	change dead material and excretory products to ammonium salts.	1
	Nitrifying bacteria	1
	change ammonium salts to nitrite	1
	then to nitrate.	1
	(Any 4 of these points)	
(c)	Chlorine kills bacteria.	1
(d)	Nitrates are absorbed into the roots and passed through the transport system of the plant to the leaves where they are used to make protein during photosynthesis.	1 1
4 (a)	150 kJ/year/m²	1

Examiner's tip 26 225 kJ/year/m² converted into 1st consumers minus 26 075 kJ/year/m² lost by 2nd consumers.

(b)	Reflection	1
	or absorption	1
	or evaporation.	1
	(Any 2)	
(c)	Respiration	1
	or excretion	1
	or death	1
	or movement	1
	or growth	1
	or reproduction.	1
	(Any 2)	
(d)	$\dfrac{1\,940\,000}{2\,000\,000} \times 100 = 97\%$	1

Examiner's tip Always show your working.

Answers to Unit 4

(e)	Greater energy loss between successive stages because the total energy loss between a producer, 1st consumer and 2nd consumer is greater than the energy loss between a producer and 1st consumer only.	1 1

5 HUMAN BIOLOGY

Question	Answer	Mark
1 (a)	The rate of height increase decreases rapidly for the first 3 years, then continues to decrease less rapidly until 12 years.	1 1

Examiner's tip — If you answered 'decreases', you would only gain 1 mark.

(b)	Puberty	1

Examiner's tip — Not adolescence. When you reach puberty you reach adolescence, but adolescence continues until the age of about eighteen, when growth slows down.

(c)	Deepening of the voice, development of pubic hair, sperm production.	3 × 1
(d)	Menstruation, breast development, pubic hair development.	2 × 1
2 (a)	Menstruation.	1
(b)	[graph with C—D, Fertilization, X marked]	1
(c)	The wall of the uterus becomes richly supplied with blood so that a placenta can develop.	1 1
(d)	It undergoes cell division and moves to the uterus through the oviduct.	1 1
(e)	If the oviducts are blocked, it will be impossible for the eggs that are shed during ovulation to reach the oviduct.	1
(f) (i)	For fertilization to take place as there is a much better chance of the sperm meeting the egg than if sperm were to be placed inside the woman's reproductive system.	1 1

Answers to Unit 5

Question			Answer	Mark
		(ii)	They undergo division and are much more likely to survive in this more advanced state of development.	1
	(g)		Test tubes are never used in the process	1
			and the baby is born naturally after being implanted in the uterus at an early stage in development.	1
	(h)		The placenta develops.	1
			The amniotic fluid surrounds the baby.	1
			The wall of the uterus becomes thicker.	1

Examiner's tip Another acceptable answer would be the development of the umbilical cord.

3	(a)	(i)	Large surface area for diffusion.	1
		(ii)	A rich blood supply to transport materials to and from the embryo.	1
	(b)		(One mark for each of three pieces of information for each gas.)	
		(i)	Carbon dioxide enters the blood from respiring cells in the embryo.	1
			It is carried as hydrogen carbonate in the blood.	1
			The hydrogen carbonate diffuses from the embryo's blood into the mother's blood (in the placenta) and then diffuses into the mother's lungs or alveoli.	1
		(ii)	Oxygen enters blood in the mother's lungs.	1
			It is carried as oxyhaemoglobin to the embryo's cells.	1
			The oxygen then leaves the embryo's blood cells to be used in respiration.	1
		(iii)	Urea enters the blood from the embryo's liver.	1
			The urea is carried in the embryo's blood plasma, and is diffused into the mother's blood plasma in the placenta.	1
			It is carried in the blood plasma to the mother's kidneys for filtration and excretion.	1

4	(a)		46	1
	(b)	(i)	2 and 3	1
		(ii)	A change in a gene or in a chromosome or in the number of chromosomes in a species.	1

Examiner's tip The word 'change' is not enough. Take notice of the two lines to write your answer.

	(c)		Subatomic particles bombard genes	1
			and alter their chemical structure.	1

Answers to Unit 5

Question	Answer	Mark

5 (a) (i)

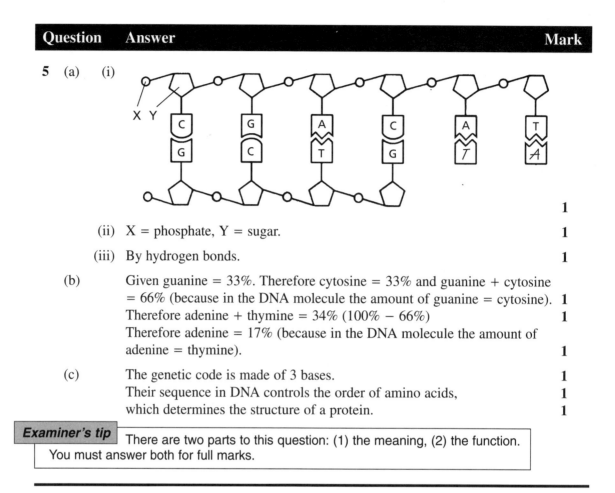

		1
(ii)	X = phosphate, Y = sugar.	1
(iii)	By hydrogen bonds.	1
(b)	Given guanine = 33%. Therefore cytosine = 33% and guanine + cytosine = 66% (because in the DNA molecule the amount of guanine = cytosine).	1
	Therefore adenine + thymine = 34% (100% − 66%)	1
	Therefore adenine = 17% (because in the DNA molecule the amount of adenine = thymine).	1
(c)	The genetic code is made of 3 bases.	1
	Their sequence in DNA controls the order of amino acids,	1
	which determines the structure of a protein.	1

Examiner's tip There are two parts to this question: (1) the meaning, (2) the function. You must answer both for full marks.

6 PLANT BIOLOGY

Question	Answer	Mark
1 (a)	To investigate whether light is needed for germination of grass seeds.	1
(b)	Oxygen	1
	A suitable temperature	1
	Water	1

Examiner's tip 'Air' is not acceptable because germination does not require any other gases found in air. 'Warmth' is not acceptable because some seeds require warmer temperatures than others. 'Dampness' is not acceptable because it could refer to humidity. Seeds require water in its liquid state.

(c)	Another box should be set up in complete darkness so that all possible conditions are investigated.	1
2 (a)	Light	1
	Carbon dioxide	1

Examiner's tip Light and carbon dioxide are both needed for photosynthesis. To confirm your ideas: the black card on leaf B will stop light and the sodium or potassium hydroxide will absorb any carbon dioxide.

76

Answers to Unit 6

Question	Answer	Mark
(b) (i)	Leaf A	1
	Leaf D	1
(ii)	Leaf A. Reason: To show the need for light. Compare leaf A with leaf B. The only difference is that the chlorophyll of leaf A is exposed to the light, while leaf B is in the dark.	1
	Leaf D. Reason: To show the need for carbon dioxide. Compare leaf D with leaf C. The only difference is that leaf D is exposed to carbon dioxide, while leaf C is not.	1

Examiner's tip A control is used to compare 'ordinary' conditions with a change in conditions.

(c)	During destarching, the plant is left in the dark for 48 hours.	1
	In the dark, starch is changed into sugar in the leaf.	1
	It is transported away in the phloem	1
	to be used in respiration.	1
		(Any 3)

Examiner's tip There are four possible points. You would be expected to mention at least 3 of the above points to gain full marks.

---

3 (a) (i)	Table 1: A	
	E	
	C	**2**
		(All correct 2 marks. Two correct 1 mark.)
	Table 2: D	
	F	1
		(Both correct 1 mark)

Examiner's tip B is the petal; this answer is not needed. There is usually one extra label, to avoid you answering them all correctly by luck. You do not need to write the name of the part, just the letter.

(ii)	Insect	1

Examiner's tip You could work this out because of the presence of petals and a nectary, the internal stigma and stamen, and also the shape of the flower.

(b) (i)	100	
	76 −	
	24 $24 \div 48 = 0.5\,cm^3/hour$	1

Examiner's tip The answer is divided by 48 because the experiment was left for 48 hours.

(ii)	Stomata (singular: stoma)	1
	To allow gases (carbon dioxide and oxygen) to diffuse into and out of the leaf.	1

Answers to Unit 6

Question	Answer	Mark

Examiner's tip It is possible to answer the second part correctly, even if you cannot remember the name stomata.

    (iii) There are more stomata in the lower surface of the leaf compared to the upper surface.   **1**

Examiner's tip If you did not know this fact you could work it out from the results. In cylinder B there was less water loss; in this cylinder the lower leaf surface was covered in vaseline.

    (iv) Any one of:
same number of leaves
similar size of leaves
all living leaves
similar positions (not too close together)
all young leaves (older leaves may have stomata blocked by dust, etc.)   **1**

    (v) The layer of oil prevents water evaporating from the cylinders.   **1**

4 (a) (i) There was relatively more water in the sugar solution than in the potato tissue and so water diffused into the potato cells   **1**
through the selectively permeable membrane.   **1**

Examiner's tip The question asked you to explain. An answer such as 'It gained +11.7%' would not gain any credit.

    (ii) There was relatively more water in the potato cells than in the sugar solution so water diffused out of the potato cells   **1**
through the selectively permeable membrane.   **1**

  (b) (i) 60 g per dm³.   **1**

    (ii) There was no change in mass of the potato so there was no net flow of water in or out of the potato because the concentration was the same on both sides of the cell membrane.   **1**

  (c) (i) The potato slices were not dried before being weighed.   **1**

    (ii) There would have been varying masses of water clinging to the outside of the potato slices.   **1**

    (iii) Dry the potato slices in a standard way, i.e. for the same time with filter paper.   **1**

  (d) The actual mass gain would not be accurate because the potato slices were not the same mass to start with.   **1**

  (e) There was no change in mass in the boiled potato because boiling would destroy the cell membrane and so it would not be selectively permeable.   **1**